Psychocinema

Theory Redux series
Series editor: Laurent de Sutter

Published Titles

Mark Alizart, *Cryptocommunism*
Armen Avanessian, *Future Metaphysics*
Franco Berardi, *The Second Coming*
Alfie Bown, *The Playstation Dreamworld*
Laurent de Sutter, *Narcocapitalism*
Diedrich Diederichsen, *Aesthetics of Pop Music*
Roberto Esposito, *Persons and Things*
Boris Groys, *Becoming an Artwork*
Graham Harman, *Immaterialism*
Helen Hester, *Xenofeminism*
Srećko Horvat, *The Radicality of Love*
Lorenzo Marsili, *Planetary Politics*
Dominic Pettman, *Infinite Distraction*
Eloy Fernández Porta, *Nomography*
Mikkel Bolt Rasmussen, *Late Capitalist Fascism*
Gerald Raunig, *Making Multiplicity*
Helen Rollins, *Psychocinema*
Avital Ronell, *America*
Nick Srnicek, *Platform Capitalism*
Grafton Tanner, *Foreverism*
Oxana Timofeeva, *Solar Politics*
Alenka Zupančič, *Disavowal*

Psychocinema

Helen Rollins

polity

First published in 2024 by Polity Press

Polity Press
65 Bridge Street
Cambridge CB2 1UR, UK

Polity Press
111 River Street
Hoboken, NJ 07030, USA

ISBN-13: 978-1-5095-6113-1
ISBN-13: 978-1-5095-6114-8 (pb)

A catalogue record for this book is available from the British Library.

Library of Congress Control Number: 2024934194

Typeset in 12.5 on 15pt Adobe Garamond
by Cheshire Typesetting Ltd, Cuddington, Cheshire
Printed and bound in Great Britain by CPI Group (UK) Ltd, Croydon

For further information on Polity, visit our website:
politybooks.com

Contents

Introduction: The Analyst's Discourse

From Opposition to Contradiction

What I aim to reveal in this book is the emancipatory potential housed in the cinematic artform. This potential is structurally analogous to the cure within psychoanalysis; namely, it can provide a space in which the viewer is able to traverse their fantasy and confront their fundamental – ontological – Lack. It is in this disturbing confrontation that individuals might be able to orient themselves differently in relation to their enjoyment, discovering a mode of desire that short-circuits our libidinal investment in capitalist Bad Infinity.

In order to excavate this potential, we must begin by seeing how cinema has been neutered by a trend within the mainstream culture of both film theory and filmmaking that has necessarily misunderstood and misused psychoanalytic ideas and that has come to serve neoliberal politics and the philosophies of identity, difference and closure, rather than the most scandalous revelation of psychoanalysis – that subjectivity is universally ambivalent and structured by Lack.

Whilst psychoanalytic theory and practice elevate, expose and explore subjective Lack as a residue of the contradictory nature of our world (as Hegel explains, Thought is the move from the abstract to the concrete) and gradually open the subject to the material reality of their life, identitarian rereadings of psychoanalysis fold existential contradiction back into oppositional ideas and abstract the subject from their material reality, a logic that accords with capitalist libido and is widely identifiable in the turn away from emancipatory politics on the Right.

Whilst it may be clear that conservative identitarianism pertains to the Master's Discourse (itself structurally comparable to that of the Capitalist), particularist theories within art and culture, reifying essence and difference, may operate according to the University Discourse. Apparently radical, this discourse obfuscates the logic of the Master within its very structure.

This book claims it is vital we return our psychoanalytic film practice and theory to the dynamic of the Analyst's Discourse. In doing so, film may come to help us challenge the ever-intensifying bad faith of our libidinal economy, which continues not only to create and justify immense precarity and subjugation but also to capture the subject at the precise moment when a dialectical, contradictory approach is perhaps most necessary.

A Poetic Logic, or A Metonymic One

Although books in film theory tend to focus on the material nature and technical quality of the film form, this text explores film's operation upon subjectivity and does so most especially via a work's narrative structure or philosophical impetus – the former itself possessing a potentially psychoanalytic, technological function.

Given the book's length, film's image is not given primacy here; nor are aesthetic features examined poetically, according to the logic of metaphor ("carrying across" – the replicating of a word's signification in another context). Rather, the text takes as a foundational premise the logic of metonymy – that a signifier's junction with another presents an explosion of infinite possibility. A film's meaning is therefore taken literally at the manifest level. It is found in the chain of signifiers presented to the viewer symbolically via the film's narrative, or in the Real of its logical contradictions. This book is therefore a philosophical one, though it claims that a Lacanian approach may have practical, material, poetic and aesthetic consequences.

The Four Discourses

Lacan developed his theory of The Four Discourses in 1969 in part as a response to what he saw as the philosophical failures of the student protests in Paris the previous year. In doing so, he may have taken inspiration from Freud's earlier insight that conscious knowledge alone cannot resolve the symptom.[1] Anticipating the rise of neoliberalism, Lacan claimed that the conscious, cultural approach taken by the students would not challenge the edifice of capitalist libido and would instead lead to a deepening and a greater obfuscation of its workings through ideology and the liberatory promises of consumer capitalism.

Whilst the Analyst's Discourse works according to the unconscious, affective and libidinal dynamics of the practice of psychoanalysis, the University Discourse makes its critiques at the level of consciousness and the cerebral. Whilst much university study does not operate according to the University Discourse – and, in fact, one of the originary premises of the university was to protect study from the undermining process of market forces – it is increasingly difficult for writers and theorists to put forward dialectical and universalist ideas within a neoliberal structure that sells research and teaching as a commodity and that accords with an oppositional, rather than a contradictory, logic.

Further, because film culture itself has become dominated not only by neoliberal market forces, but by those of a potentially new formation of capitalist economy, emerging from the collapsed contradictions of neoliberalism itself – a form of state-sponsored monopoly "socialism" that protects corporations from the near-zero global rate of profit – there has been, in this sphere, an even greater prevalence of oppositional theories that mystify what is going on.

Film itself, however, because it operates on affect and the visceral and – more importantly – on libido and desire, may still be able – like psychoanalysis as practice – to raise the unconsciousness of the viewer and expose them to the universal structure of their subjectivity in ways that are potentially politically significant.

Contradictory Film Theory

Cinematic practice and theory are faced with increasing limitations, both conscious and unconscious, engendered by worsening material conditions. The creation of challenging, dialectical and non-oppositional work is nearly impossible within the contours of our current economy. Whilst filmmaking in these conditions has its challenges, it may still be possible to readdress the analysis of films with insight and productivity.

Instead of consciously striving to excavate the "hidden" meaning of a film, for example, we can elevate – through the Analyst's Discourse – the dynamics of the Real at play within the functioning of the machine of cinema, digesting them into the shared language of the Symbolic Order to understand how these dynamics direct our subjectivity and desire. We can treat the visual representation of film not as confirmation of the cultural biases we already hold to be true, but rather as the higher-order expression of a wider nexus of phenomena that underpin our world, an attunement to which can constantly challenge our assumptions and leave us open to the generative dialectic of our universe, which itself may lead to a reformulation of material conditions.

This book argues for a return to an openness toward contradiction in the understanding of film, which – it claims – is the impulse of the psychoanalytic method. It argues that cinema is a tool that can help us in this reorientation, both as an artform that operates upon us and as an object of study. It posits that popularized film theory has misunderstood the radical import of universal contradiction in the practice and theory of psychoanalysis and has focused on particularisms which pose no challenge to capitalist ideology, but are in fact determinative of its persistence.

Immanent Transcendence

Film as a technology was created at the end of the nineteenth century. Early viewers of cinema wondered at its apparent magic. The true "magic" of cinema is perhaps found not in its mechanistic capacity to convincingly replicate reality but in its ability to generate an affective excess within the viewer – a residue, like prayer, that is more than the sum of its constitutive parts.

The relationship between film and the viewer can function like the relationship of the analyst and the analysand in the practice of psychoanalysis, with a libidinal energy oscillating between each party according to the dynamics of transference, exposing a Lack in subjectivity that is experienced, by the subject, as something substantive. In Kristeva's words, this dynamic is experienced as something like "an immanent transcendence here on earth."[2]

This book will lay out and explain the ways in which the structure of the machine of film has endowed it with this fortuitous capacity. It claims that, whilst this capacity is concealed in all kinds of films, a sensitive approach by filmmakers may allow for a higher-order activation of this dynamic, animating the viewer's subjectivity to produce an unconscious insight as to the contradictory nature of their subjective constitution.

Universalist Film

Film and psychoanalysis point to a dynamic within human subjectivity that is universal, an essential (k)not that exists across every form of identity and desire. The universal quality of film has been commented upon by many theorists, including Badiou, who says that "[c]inema opens all the arts, it weakens their aristocratic, complex and composite quality. It delivers this simplified opening to images of unanimous existence. As painting without painting, music without music, novel without subjects, theater reduced to the charm of actors, cinema ensures the popularization of all the arts. This is why its vocation is universal."[3]

There is a collectivity that marks film, from the way it is produced to the way it is watched, even within the constraints of the particularist pressures of contemporary capitalism. However, it is perhaps the capacity that film has to expose the viewer to the Real of their desire – that they are constituted by a fundamental Lack, that they are, in the words of Žižek, universally "less than nothing"[4] – that is its most radical, universalist dynamic.

A recognition of this universal constitution-by-Lack may have political consequences. It undermines the logic of the market system, which relies on the false promise of possible fulfillment via the achievement of a commodity. When the subject transforms this truth from the register of the Real to that of the Symbolic, they understand that there is no beyond of Lack for themself or any other subject, that the economic reality that entraps them relies on a false promise that can never be fulfilled. Through this insight, a philosophical opening may occur within the nexus of our collective libidinal economy, and the reconstitution of the material reality of our world becomes a possibility – a material reality that seems to sharply resist, and even adapt to, conscious attempts to overcome it.

Capitalist Utopianism

Capitalism is a mode of production that relies on a denial of the universal, fundamental, generative force that is Lack, whilst exploiting it. Because capitalist logic can only tolerate the contradiction of Lack when it is repressed and denied, it must retreat from the conscious acknowledgment of Lack as a phenomenon and turn toward a logic of opposition.

Opposition is a logic that acts as a parasite on Lack, while denying its existence.

Capitalist logic is a utopianism that promises existential purity, the inevitable completion of desire and the absolution of Lack, even when – as Marx points out – it is constantly under threat from its own internal contradictions.[5] In fact, capitalism derives its power precisely from its failure to deliver on these impossible promises. It casts the fundamental Lack that constitutes human subjectivity as a contingent, corrigible loss that can be defeated. Within capitalism, alienation is not something constitutive, but rather a contingent event that can be overcome.

Capitalism cannot make good on the purifying promise of the commodities it offers because it relies on the purchasing of more products by unfulfilled subjects who imagine these products will eventually assuage them. Instead of exposing this fundamental contradiction within the economy, capitalism must repress it, forcing the capitalist subject to enter into an oppositional, enemy-oriented logic to excuse the system's own failings.

The repression of this contradiction leads to existential disquiet, emotional suffering and extreme violence. The poor suffer through the inadequate distribution of resources to achieve a reasonable standard of living, through the "meritocratic" and "philanthropic" cover stories of corporate capitalism that cast blame upon them for their material position, and through the physical violence with which any challenge to these contradictions is repressed. The rich suffer existentially. Whilst able to appropriate the monetary benefits of surplus value, they are constantly confronted by the blunt impotence of material things to assuage their existential Lack, often experiencing a melancholic disengagement from the reality of their life or, very often, a consequential – though contradictory – drive to accrue more.

This suffering, a result of the repressed illogic of our economic system, emerges as cultural phenomena that psychoanalysis terms "symptoms." In Seminar XXIII, Lacan explores the implications of his neologism "sinthome" or "saintly man" (a play on the French word for symptom – "symptôme") in reference to psychosis.[6] Whilst "sinthome" more specifically expresses the contradiction that cannot be undone without the undoing of the very edifices of subjectivity, by drawing out the linguistic similarity between "sinthome" and "symptôme," Lacan suggests that symptoms can – if interpreted correctly – expose us productively to the truths of our economic system that we are at such pains to deny, like a prophet.

Film, by exposing our reality back to us, can reveal – intentionally or not – the symptoms of our collective disquiet and help us to confront them, digest and resolve them in generative and enjoyable ways.

Film as Philosophy

Capitalism operates according to a binary, oppositional logic which attempts to nullify existential Lack and contingently absolve it with commoditized solutions. Art is a phenomenon that houses contradiction within it, without any attempt to eradicate it. It is this phenomenal ambivalence that makes art art and distinguishes it from the conscious call-to-action of propaganda.

Although capitalism must rationalize contradiction and mute the most powerful dynamics within art, favoring and foregrounding "art" that can be folded into the constraints of the Master's Discourse, there is a force to film that seems to transcend the market forces that are driven to quell it. It is a current that collides against the Master's Discourse and can productively position the viewer toward their Gaze of Lack, mobilizing them toward a dialectical encounter with the contours of their very desire.

The "grand narratives" of the structurally riven filmic form have been criticized throughout the history of film theory for supporting the totalitarian logic of capitalism. However, it is perhaps this very structure of film that allows for a productive confrontation with Lack through transference. Here, a libidinal investment by the viewer occurs through the misguided belief in the promise of closure and, as in psychoanalysis, the film may employ and exploit this "mistake" in order to expose the viewer to the contradictory nature of their desire. Further, the narratively taut film – consciously unaware of its logical contradictions

– may expose to us, in relief, the symptoms of our own society. If philosophy is the tarrying with the contradictions at the heart of the universe, film may act as a powerful philosophical technology.

The Analyst's Discourse Makes Hysterics of Us All

Žižek posits in *The Pervert's Guide to Ideology* and *The Pervert's Guide to Cinema* that "cinema is the ultimate pervert art."[7] It could be worth suggesting an alternative idea – that cinema has the capacity to make hysterics of us all.

Whilst biological sex is a factor in the subject's first birth into matter, sexuation is a result of their second birth into language. It refers to the development of one's subjective relationship to sexuality and to Lack, which engenders it. Lacan posited two primary forms of sexuation, which some have called Imposture and Masquerade (more commonly termed the Not-All). Whilst the first is gendered as "masculine" and the second "feminine," these are symbolic forms of identification and do not reflect biological reality or subjective structure as a matter of course.[8] In Imposture, the subject identifies with the phallus, an imagined symbol of power and completeness – there exists an imagined ideal beyond castration. In Masquerade, the subject identifies with the absence of the phallus and experiences an existential sense of incompleteness (though may come to embody the phallus for the Impostor). This is why Hysteria (the "female"-gendered neurosis, nothing to do with the maligned image of a "hysteric" in common cultural parlance) is understood, by Lacan, to be more proximate with a political potential in that a hysteric recognizes "her" Lack more readily. Masculinity may be experienced as real; femininity feels the truth of its contradiction.

The hysteric is sensitive to the contradictions that mark their subjectivity and the world. These contradictions point to a fundamental break in reality itself, a break that makes reality possible in the first place. This sensitivity endows the hysteric with an impulse to question the authority of the Master, which may have political and emancipatory results, as long as the critical process is not itself captured by the unitary promise of capitalism – a hallmark of the "progress" narratives of neoliberalism, which has come to create a universe of apparently "castrated" bosses and movie stars.

For Lacan, despite the distinct modes of sexuation and infinite categories of identity and desire that can shape and form the subject, there is a "dimension of hysteria latent in every kind of human being in the world."[9] This latent dimension is what makes possible an opening toward the emancipatory confrontation with Lack in all subjects, which cinema may be able to make manifest via its very structure. This latent dimension is that which is political in its collision with film, that which McGowan refers to when he says that "the greatest films aesthetically are the greatest films politically."[10]

When Žižek suggests that cinema is a pervert's art, he is referring to the way in which film can teach us how and what to desire. This is the same logic that marks advertisements under consumer capitalism, the rise of which is so magically captured in Matthew Weiner's television series *Mad Men*. It is a perverse logic that makes perverts of those on whom it operates by making them feel they are certain – temporarily at least – of how and what they desire.

The Analyst's Discourse sensitizes the subject to a universal Lack at the heart of our existence, a generative disquiet that haunts the human subject from their first breath to their last. It cuts across class and identity, speaking to the possibility of radically altering our political economy and challenging the ideological edifice that necessitates and endorses the subjugation, exclusion and exploitation of given groups. In other words, the Analyst's Discourse hystericizes the subject, leading them to question the orthodoxy of the day and generate knowledge, like the scientist approaching her experiment from a place of doubt, letting go of all suppositions, in order to be challenged by the possibility of the new.

Watching a film – and reading a film in a truly analytic way – confronts us with the ambivalent truth of our desire in all its inconsistencies, as well as the universal Lack that sustains it and around which we, as capitalist subjects, may collectively reorient ourselves in order to transform the material structure of our society.

To confront the Real of our subjectivity is traumatic, but it is productive. It may offer us the philosophical approach necessary to stand outside of the libidinal dynamic that entraps us. Ideology protects us from the radical insight of psychoanalysis as to the impossible structure of our desire. Our addiction to ideology leads us to live in unreasonable, unproductive and unequal ways that do not meet the dialectical nature of our reality.

Political Revolution, Philosophical Revolution

Crises in the material conditions of society are easily taken up by reactionary forces and weaponized in the service of oppositional agendas; however, they also house the potential to unleash an emancipatory event. Such emancipatory events, however, will themselves become ossified over time, becoming part of new economic systems that themselves must be enveloped in the dance of affirmation, negation and negation of negation.

Dialectical Materialism is a commitment to the ongoing effort to expose the contradiction as it manifests in the present epoch, not so as to overcome it, but rather to transform it. Not in some postmodern Bad Infinity in which we are always open to a future that never arrives, but ultimately to reach the point where we realize that the Real is not a messiah that is to come, but one that has already arrived. In other words, that contradiction is never finally overcome, but recognized as an ontological reality always already among us.

Desire and fantasy are structured by material conditions and by collective libido. They are ways by which the human subject manages their Lack and psychically deals with the material conditions of their life, which themselves can be too difficult to consciously bear. Because film brings the contours of human desire into relief, because the desire of the viewer speaks through the film that they watch, a philosophical – analytic – study of these dynamics can expose us to the material structure of our economy that capitalism is so at pains to mystify.

If confessional religion was the opium of the subject in past orders of societal organization, the capitalist orientation of desire toward closure can be understood as contemporary religiosity, even in its most "atheistic" manifestation. God, for Lacan, today resides in the unconscious drive toward the solution of absolutes. And the confidence of critique mystifies the persistence of this dynamic.

For Nietszche, god died and his shadow was cast on cave walls for 1,000 years.[11] Perhaps film can be conceived of as this shadowed projection, playing with and exposing our fantasies, which are religious insofar as they protect us from the Lack at the core of our existence. A theological illumination and analysis of this shadowed projection and of the subjective fantasies it exploits may yield political and philosophical insights.

By confronting the subject with the fundamental, productive Lack in desire, film can reveal the illogic of ideology, its religiosity and the ways in which it enslaves and entraps us. In this way, film accords with the logic of Marx's analogy of the living flower,[12] sensitizing the subject to the ersatz flowers that decorate their chains and encouraging them to pluck the living flower, which grows in the grit and grime of the R/real world.

The soils that grow the living flower are born of the same antagonisms that generate subjectivity. The living flower is one that we must cultivate according to the conscious workings of reality – collectively, collaboratively, politically. Thus, though film might appear loftily detached from the baseness of the practical world via its commitment to movie stars, its focus on fantasy and the make-believe of plot, it may lead us back, via the transferential process, to the ordinary unhappiness of normality, to a socialist libidinal economy, or even perhaps a communist one – not despite these things, but because of them.

Psychocinema

"Ne pas céder sur son désir" – *The Devils*

The architecture of film actively positions the viewer toward a confrontation with the Lack in desire. Likewise, the practice of psychoanalysis gradually confronts the analysand with the contradictory nature of their desire, mobilizing their libido away from a totalitarian capitalist logic that promises a fulfillment that is logically impossible, and toward an enjoyment of the productive impossibility of their desire as such.

Lacan illustrates the contradictory nature of desire in his famous passage from Seminar VII – "la seule chose dont on [peut] être coupable, au moins dans la perspective analytique, c'est d'avoir cédé sur son désir."[1] The latter part of this phrase is deliberately obscure and has been rendered various ways in English, sometimes missing its syntactical ambivalence. Dennis Porter translates this passage as – "the only thing of which one can be guilty . . . is of having given ground relative to one's desire,"[2] which captures Lacan's paradoxical phrasing. The use of the preposition "sur" by Lacan after the verb "céder" (to yield) is unusual; it generally takes the preposition "à" – to give oneself over to something. The verb can also take an object, followed by the indirect pronoun, for example "céder le passage à quelqu'un" (to give [right of] way to someone else).

Porter's "giving ground" echoes the ambivalence of the verb "céder"; his "relative to" captures the obscurity of Lacan's use of the preposition "sur."

The statement can be interpreted as an indication that one should not give oneself over to one's desire – one should not "yield" to it or "give ground," allow its encroachment, in one's life. On the other hand, the statement can be read as a command to not let one's desire pass one by – like a vehicle at a stop or "yield" sign, giving way to passing traffic, putting distance between oneself and one's desire.

For Lacan, there is no fulfillment in the completion of desire, but there is no fulfillment in abstinence either. Lacan is therefore neither a utopian capitalist, promising transcendence in the achievement of a goal or the attainment of a commodity, nor a reactionary conservative, promising an inverse transcendence in the purity of non-desire.

For the subject, the truth of the ambivalence of their desire is not an easy one to digest. Confronting it can be traumatic as it points to the lacking nature of the universe and the subject's existence within it as nothing more than a symptom of that Lack. In psychoanalytic terms, a raw, unmediated confrontation with this truth is an encounter with the Real.

To chip away at the Real in small doses through the process of Symbolization, to come to terms with it, is productive in terms of both the psychic health of the individual and the political well-being of the collective. Film has the capacity to confront the viewer with the Real of their desire. It does so, like psychoanalysis, in manageable doses. And it does so as a medium that is enjoyable and – at times – comforting for the subject.

Psychoanalysis owes much to Hegel in its understanding that desire is not unique in its contradictory status, but rather contradictory precisely because it emerges from matter, which is itself divided. Hegel anticipated the hypothesis of the Big Bang by over a century. According to the theory of some cosmologists – proximate to the ethos of Hegel's work in its postulation of a fundamental asymmetry at its heart – a single point in the universe became so blisteringly hot and dark and infinitely dense that the forces inside it became mathematically indiscernible from their opposite. In a sudden moment of contradiction, all energies at this infinitely small point were redirected outward, backfiring with such an intensity that matter was generated from nothing and countless galaxies were cast outward onto the vast, black canvas of the sky.

Although there is no mind to recollect this moment, every rock, cell, every form of consciousness and self-consciousness in our world carries a meticulous account of it, something that was referred to by Hegel through his insight that "substance [is] as subject."[3]

Matter is contradictory, as are the workings of the mind. The difference is that, whilst the contradiction of matter is not self-conscious, the contradiction of mind emerges from the contradiction of matter and is the experience of the universe witnessing its own contradictions. Quantum theory identifies the contradiction that marks matter; psychoanalysis explicates the generation of self-consciousness through the division of matter and is concerned with the sufferings of the subject, unable to confront and digest their own contradictory nature.

The Devils (dir. Ken Russell, 1971) depicts this impossible nature of desire. Whilst the capitalist promise that there can be a fulfillment of desire is a fallacy, *The Devils* shows what can happen when the subject chooses, or is forced, to turn away from their desire altogether.

Repression is not to do with not getting what one wants, but rather to do with defending oneself against the knowledge of how – and potentially what – one desires. To acknowledge one's own desire and not give ground relative to it, to make consciously Symbolized – rather than purely unconscious – sacrifices in terms of that desire when living in a community of people with diverse desires of their own, by using one's discernment and negotiating with the dialectical reality of the world relative to one's desire, one becomes a political subject. This is impossible under a repressive regime like the one depicted in *The Devils*.

The film is set during Cardinal Richelieu's France, as the nation emerged from the Middle Ages and was plagued by a mysterious pestilence, understood to be satanic – a terrifying eruption of the Real. Social anxiety was managed through sexual purity, acting as an individualist stand-in for a failed societal repression of the darkest matters of the universe – in this case, a lack of scientific understanding. As a returned repressed, sexual purity became reactionary – emerging with a consequential, redoubled force.

Sex is underpinned by a fantasy structure that emerges in childhood as a response to the mystery of the Other's desire. This mystery is the undefinable Lack in the subjectivity of the Other and is traumatic because it points to the unmanageable contradiction of the universe as such. Sex is therefore experienced as impure for the reactionary, who tries to manage the ambivalence of the universe and their subjectivity by casting out the necessary, generative contradiction within themselves onto a scapegoated Other. The reactionary subject may repress their own sexuality in an attempt to deny their own subjective impurity, under the gaze of an unkind god, for example, who must be bargained with and appeased lest Satan penetrate the world of the living.

When repression occurs at the level of the unconscious, the affect related to the repressed phenomenon returns, attached to other phenomena, creating chaos and dissatisfaction that are unmeasured and out of control. *The Devils* was made at the peak of sexual openness, shortly after the sexual revolution of '68. It is filmed in a carnival of psychedelic lighting, extravagant costume and camp production design, which – at first blush – seem antithetical to the subject matter at hand, but in fact underscore the power of the returned repressed, erupting as it does in displays of great sexual intensity, at least as excessive as the force with which the complexity and Lack in sex are held down.

The puritanical nuns of the film are utopians who imagine the world can be purified of complexity and contradiction. Their ideological approach necessitates a scapegoat whom they can imagine is uncastrated, overflowing with sexual excess, and who can hold within their image all the sexual uncleanliness of the society of which they aim to be absolved.

Urbain Grandier is their chosen scapegoat. The crime of being extremely handsome is the catalyst for the contingent petrification of devilhood within him. The nuns are, in reality, experiencing an intolerable division within themselves – a complexity of sexual desire that cannot be borne. Grandier becomes the accidental emblem of his society's unrest, capturing the floating, repressed energy within the community of nuns. He is the contingent gristle of the Real.

Like the stereotypical nun within cultural history who imagines they have a libidinal relationship with the crucified Christ, the nuns identify with the sexual desire they project onto Grandier. The delusion that they have had forced sexual relations with him allows them to deal with their own unrecognized desires and justifies the Inquisition's arrest, torture and ritual purging of Grandier from the collective. Through this dynamic, the nuns are regressing to a stage of psychic development that takes place in early infancy. It is a moment that Hegel refers to as the

Beautiful Soul[4] and that Klein labels the paranoid schizoid position.[5]

During its early years, the child must go through a primary repression in order to generate an ego that helps them navigate the world. With language, the child's ego is built and with it comes contradiction at the level of their subjectivity. Within the paranoid schizoid position, the subject attempts to manage these contradictions by projecting them outward. Though Klein posits the position is adopted in the second half of the first year, young children continue to integrate and manage these subjective contradictions throughout their infancy – the little boy obsessed with dinosaurs, toys that could annihilate everything if only they were real. The little girl playing the innocent princess, scared at night because of the big, hairy monster under her bed. This is a logic of absolutes – good and bad, black and white. It is a war of all against all.

For Klein, the depressive is able to tolerate ambiguity. In the film, it is Grandier who embodies this depressive position. His community at Loudon tolerates both Protestant and Catholic. He doesn't hold to interpretations of the Bible that the authoritarian regime demands of him.

He lives with shades of gray. The nuns, however, seem to inhabit a paranoid schizoid position. Grandier becomes the unwitting receiver of their projective identification.

Whilst primary repression is a necessary stage of early childhood and whilst we need barriers to that which we desire in order to conjure that very desire, excessive repressions that nullify the productive contradictions of life can create greater torment than the ambivalence they seek to resolve. *The Devils* exploits the affective power of the horror form, and even pornography, to express – viscerally – the complexity and ambivalence of desire, subjectivity and sex, perhaps most especially the unconscious force with which the subject protects themself against the contradictions that generate them.

The Devils shows that film is able to tolerate and house contradiction, playing form against content, revealing the dialectic of a character's split subjectivity, reflecting back to the audience the contradictions that are the foundations of their own reality.

The Alienation of Alienation – *The Green Ray*

A common, and important, critique leveled at capitalism is that it alienates the subject from their true desires when forced to undertake paid work to sustain their survival. Whilst this critique is valid, it misses the multiplicity and uncertainty of the subject's desire in the first instance – the question of what they would desire to do with their time if they were totally free to make the most of it.

The market system does indeed alienate the subject, but it does so most fundamentally by alienating them from the contradictory nature of their desire – the fact the human subject is alienated at the outset from themself. Marx is a philosopher who explores the secondary alienation instigated by the capitalist system. Hegel and Lacan are philosophers who explore the ways in which subjects are not at one with themselves.

The instability of human desire, and the impotence of objects and phenomena in the fulfillment of it, are disturbing for the human subject since they point to the lacking nature of the universe and the fact that the subject emerges from less than nothing. To recognize the truth of these factors, however, is ultimately liberatory because it allows the subject to have a greater understanding of the complex nature of the world in which they live and it allows them to live more productively in relation to its contradictions.

The practice of psychoanalysis gradually helps the subject to confront these truths and to accept them. Bion refers to this dynamic as one of "alphabetization,"[6] or a process of "digestion."[7] The acceptance of these truths works against the grain of market logic, which relies on the libidinal investment of the subject in the transcendental power of a singular commodity to meet and fulfill a clearly defined desire.

The Green Ray (1986) is a film by Éric Rohmer that confronts the viewer with the alienation its protagonist, Delphine, experiences in relation to her own desire. After a break-up, Delphine is left alone in Paris whilst the city empties for the month of August. Multiple friends and family members offer Delphine different options. She is paralyzed by the multiplicity of the offers and – free to choose – is confused by what she wants.

Delphine goes from one holiday to the next, in Cherbourg, the Alps and Biarritz, finding herself constantly dissatisfied by contingent factors that do not seem to hold up against an unarticulated perfect holiday she imagines she might enjoy.

In the final part of the film, Delphine overhears an elderly man discussing a meteorological phenomenon – a rare flash of green that occurs on the horizon at sunset. According to the Jules Verne novel of the same name, if one catches the green light and gazes into it, one understands one's desires and sees the thoughts of those close by.

Captured by the mystery and promise of the green ray, Delphine takes a man she has just met to wait for the green ray at sunset. Together they witness it. She experiences a brief moment of excitement. But the question as to whether she will receive the answer to her desire remains unresolved.

The viewer, having identified with Delphine's desire throughout the film, is let down in their expectation of closure along with her – a process that is analogous, in the longer term, to the cure in psychoanalysis.

The Trauma of Jouissance – *Citizen Kane*

In his early writings, Freud indicates that the subject is driven by two oppositional forces: the reality principle and the pleasure principle. Whilst the subject might logically seek gratification in pleasure, avoiding pain, they must temper their pleasure-seeking desires with the demands of material reality and the constraints of living in community with others. This is an insight that he later complexifies in *Beyond the Pleasure Principle*, recognizing that there is a supremacy of drive within the subject, a propensity to often seek out pain rather than pleasure.

Before Freud, Schopenhauer tells us that "life swings like a pendulum backwards and forwards between pain and boredom."[8] For Schopenhauer, the subject is caught in a quagmire of, on the one hand, experiencing depression if their desires are not fulfilled and, on the other, experiencing melancholy when they are confronted with the impotence of the object of their desire in overcoming existential Lack when they are.

Whilst both thinkers describe the difficulty of human desire in a reality that can never seem to meet it, psychoanalysis in particular is a theory and practice that attempts to address the paradoxical phenomenon that is generated for the human subject in their perpetual oscillation between the two positions that Schopenhauer describes.

In their movement between their depression in being deprived of the object of desire and their melancholy in getting it, the subject experiences a strange enjoyment that psychoanalysts term "jouissance." The difficulties that the subject has in recognizing this paradoxical pleasure is what often leads them to psychoanalysis via symptoms that have emerged as a return of the repression they have enacted upon the contradiction in their desire.

"Repression" is often overused within the culture as a descriptor solely for the suppression of sexual desires. In psychoanalytic terms, the word is more polyvalent and can refer to the ways in which the subject represses the contradiction at the level of any of their desires.

Sex and sexuality have a privileged position in psychoanalysis, however, because the fantasy and the act expose quite clearly the structure of the human subject's contradictory subjectivity. The given mode of desiring that each subject has – unique in its own way according to the infinite potentiality of Lack – exemplifies a fundamental fantasy that grounds the subject's phenomenological experience and understanding of the world. Rather than being the specific driving force of culture – something that is elevated because it is undivided, unlike everything else – sex itself is a response to Lack, an attempt by the semi-linguistic child to understand the contradiction they encounter in desire and the traumatic encounter with the subjectivity and sexuality of their primary caregivers.

All sexualities are marked by a universal contradiction. Sexual desire is traumatic in that it directly foregrounds the Lack in the universe. Sexual repression can be both an attempt to escape the complexity of desire in monk-like abstinence and also a belief in the transcendent power of sex to unify the subject in oneness. In this way, some of the most apparently sexually "liberated" subjects may in fact be the most sexually repressed.

Humans repress the ambivalence of desire and its resultant jouissance because they prefer the soothing alternative that is the logic of ideology, religiosity and capitalism: a possible ecstasy in oneness. As the Lacanian writer Vakhtang Gomelauri puts it, the subject is so reticent to confront the Lack in their desire – itself an emergence of the Lack in the universe – that they have "a tendency to desire symbolic stability even at the cost of [their] life."[9]

The trauma of jouissance is addressed in Orson Welles' 1941 masterpiece *Citizen Kane*. The film begins as Kane utters the word "Rosebud" on his deathbed, gazing into a snowglobe. This utterance instigates a retrospective investigation by a journalist, Thompson, to discover the meaning of the word.

Thompson speaks to Kane's butler, Raymond, who informs him of an event he witnessed during which Kane similarly uttered the mysterious word.

During this episode, Kane destroyed his ex-wife Susan's bedroom after she left him. In a fit of rage, Kane came upon the snowglobe, suddenly falling calm and saying the word "Rosebud." Raymond tells Thompson that he has no idea of the word's significancc. Sincc nonc of Thompson's other interviews has yielded any information, he concludes that "Rosebud" will forever remain an enigma.

As the film closes, Kane's belongings are gathered and destroyed. A sledge is found amongst the dead man's objects and is thrown into a furnace. As it burns, the word "Rosebud" is visible upon it. The audience learns that this was the sledge Kane was playing with on the snowy day on which his childhood ended at eight years old, the day he was introduced to a banker named Thatcher, who would come to control his estate and assume his guardianship. Upon meeting Thatcher, the little boy Kane hit him with his sledge and tried to run away.

For Kane, "Rosebud" represents the childhood that he lost. Like Eden for Adam and Eve or the mother's breast for the child deprived of suckling, "Rosebud" takes on a tantalizing quality for him precisely because it can never be retrieved. The sledge, for Kane, embodies this magical, lost universe. In psychoanalytic terms, it is a "lost object." Since it is impossible and irretrievable, Kane's childhood can never disappoint him: he can never attain it so it can never let him down, never fail to fulfill him in his desire.

This magical quality is an excess in reality generated as a surplus by the impossibility of contradiction itself. It is an example of the way in which the subject experiences the world as transcendent precisely because it is not. Lacan named this unobtainable depth dimension within the object of desire "objet petit a." The subject will never be able to touch this impossible depth within reality contained in the object of their desire, but they organize their desire around it and experience jouissance in their attempt to reach it and their inevitable inability to do so.

In his 2013 book *Enjoying What We Don't Have,*[10] McGowan explores how a conscious understanding of jouissance can allow the subject to acknowledge the excess in their desire inspired by what they do not or cannot have, allowing them to experience satisfaction in an aspect of their life they might otherwise find painful.

Whilst this might in the first instance appear to be a punitive logic since it appears to focus on not having rather than having, it in fact foregrounds the productive ways in which the subject is inspired by Lack. Kane is miserable because he feels a sense of loss for a moment he can never retrieve. An alternative may have been possible for him: to recognize that the magical dimension of life, that which animates it and makes it worth living, is only possible because of its material impossibility. It is not only the case, in life, that there is no light without dark, no good without bad, but also that the interplay between light and dark generates an excess in experience that cannot be obtained but can be enjoyed.

To embrace the impossibility within the object of desire is to love it. Whilst the miser experiences the impossibility of the object as a contingent loss, constantly accruing more and more objects because these objects continue to fail to fulfill them, the lover embraces the unknown within the object or individual they desire, enjoying the ever greater depths that emerge through them because of their infinite impossibility.

Though each form of subjectivity and desire is distinct, based on the contingent experience of the subject in their early years in relation to their Lack, the fundamental logic of the generation of subjectivity is universal. Every subject – speaking or physically non-verbal, though overwritten by the signifier – is shaped by Lack and shares a universal characteristic of non-belonging because of it. To recognize this psychoanalytic universality is to subjectivize and humanize everyone, undermining the logic of capitalism, which relies on an imagined non-division in the subjectivity of certain groups to justify their exclusion and exploitation as non-subjects.

In this way, since film may have the capacity to work alongside the practice and philosophy of psychoanalysis to expose the viewer toward a productive acceptance of the universal Lack in their desire, its effects upon the subject are political.

Bad Infinity – *Another Round*

The contradictory nature of desire is traumatic for the subject because it points to a wider truth about our world and our position as subjects within it – that we are alone in the universe, that there is no undivided authority and that we emerge from the contradiction in matter as such. It also undermines the economic edifice of our reality, which promises fulfillment, but can never achieve it, because it aims to meet an undivided Lack that does not exist.

In this way, the relationship of the subject of capitalism with capitalism's commodities is that of the addict with their means of achieving psychic oblivion. Like the alcoholic who soothes an unarticulated ("a-diction," unspeaking) existential trauma with the promise of ecstasy in oblivion, the capitalist can never overcome their Lack and must continue to seek out stronger and more intense versions of their object of fulfillment until the attempted cure becomes poisonous. Addicted as we are to the promise of the commodity, the market system has generated historically high levels of inequality and has failed to steward the planet that it exploits as its primary resource. Our attempted cure to our collective Lack has become poisonous.

For the alcoholic, drinking is not the sole problem, but rather – in the first place – the attempted solution to a problem they cannot otherwise confront. Becoming sober is a traumatic process because it means the removal of the very thing helping the individual to avoid confrontation with an immensely difficult part of their life. But it is only through giving up the addiction that they can begin to confront the trauma they bear and address it.

Since the promise of the commodity mystifies the divided nature of desire and the universe, the human is at pains to forgo it because the dialectical insight revealed in its absence may be too traumatic to bear.

In this way, the logic of capitalism operates according to Hegel's concept of Bad Infinity, which mystifies a confrontation of the subject with the dialectical insight of Absolute Knowing. Here, the subject's desperation to overcome contradiction leads them to buy into promises of various kinds, but these promises can never defeat the presence of contradiction in the subject's life because it is foundational to their very existence. The commodity never meets the subject's need and leads them to a repeated drive forward that never brings them to their desired destination.

A recent film that explores the logic of addiction is *Another Round* (2020) by Thomas Vinterberg. Here, four teachers – Tommy, Peter, Nikolaj and Martin – struggle with the drudgery of teaching high school students. They discuss a theory that when slightly drunk – with a blood-alcohol content of 0.05 percent – one feels more relaxed, happy and creative and one's capacity to function well in society is not undermined. The friends engage in an experiment to see whether they can sustain this perfect blood-alcohol balance and whether doing so will allow them to finally enjoy their lives.

Since, at first, the alcohol improves their experience of life, they are carried away by the promise of more. They increase the measurement to 0.1 percent and soon find themselves drinking to oblivion. As their lives slip into disarray, Peter, Nikolaj and Martin decide to abstain from alcohol, but Tommy continues to drink. He sails out to sea with his old dog, drunk, and drowns.

One of the important aspects of this film is that it is not punitive in its study of alcoholism. Rather, it points to the human issues at play in addiction, as they are in all psychic symptoms. Its attitude to alcohol is as much celebratory as it is disparaging. It handles the tragedy and triumph of the human subject in their pursuit of soothing and betterment as its characters simultaneously make spirited attempts to animate their lives and drown out the complexity of their experience.

The Tics and Grimaces of the Universe – *The Last Supper*

Hegel's *Phenomenology* identifies a foundational contradiction across all history, charting the presence and deepening of contradiction from not-at-oneness at the level of matter of rocks and rain to the divided nature of animal consciousness and the lacking structure of human self-consciousness. Within the text, he also charts the deepening of contradiction across human civilizational development. Each societal structure has attempted to manage and overcome the foundational contradiction of the universe. It is the failure of each formation to do so that leads to a newer, more modern form of civilization. Each civilization represses the essential contradiction of life at a level more unconscious than the one before.

Perhaps the most famous – and most misunderstood – expression of civilizational contradiction in Hegel's *Phenomenology* is the Master–Slave Dialectic, present in Greco-Roman society. Whilst in common cultural parlance this example is said to represent unjust power dynamics, Hegel's critique is more foundational, exploring the importance of recognition to subjectivity. A vital phenomenon in the psychoanalytic encounter, recognition – or a lack of recognition – is that which underpins society's ideological impetus to include, exclude or subjugate an individual or class: in other words, to weaponize its power and to justify its misuse.

The phenomenon of the scapegoat emerges as a result of the subject's desire to nullify existential Lack by turning toward impossible visions of existential purity. The scapegoat is the necessary obstacle that "contingently" prevents the subject from reaching their desired transcendence and preserves it, since encountering it would confront the subject with its inability to solve the Lack in their subjectivity and the universe. The scapegoat is rendered such via the collective's inability to recognize their dialectical humanity – the universal division that exists in all subjects.

In Hegel's example, citizens are believed to be subjects, capable of thought and reason, but slaves are not. Slaves are the outsiders who bear the Lack in civilization that cannot be ideologically tolerated – they are the societal scapegoat.

Though the citizen class may have conceived of themselves as subjects who were whole and complete and thus capable of thought and reason, in fact this capacity was indicative of subjective division. Only as divided subjects could they speak and thus think and therefore be capable of discernment. On the other hand, the slave was deemed "less evolved" than the citizen-subject and thus – according to the misguided logic – more lacking and less capable of thought and reason, even though it is universal Lack that makes possible the process of sensation, thought, speech and discernment. For Zupančič, the human subject is the contradiction of our world witnessing itself – the subject embodies the "tics and grimaces" of the universe.[11]

Though their position as Other provided the slave with a unique understanding as to the workings of the society from which they were excluded, they were assumed to be unable to offer a vision of it. Thus was lost a productive insight into the center that the society itself could not see.

Therefore, Greco-Roman society was plagued by a solipsistic Master's Discourse whose logic accorded with Bad Infinity. The Master's logic is conservative. Within the logic of the conservative is always housed the seeds of its own destruction. The conservative attempts to preserve the stability of the center by protecting it from the generative power of change only possible through Lack. As McGowan frequently indicates,[12] whilst Adorno claimed a principal flaw of the "totalitarian" society was its drive to universalize, this society is in fact never total enough because it cannot tolerate and must exclude Lack. It is therefore unable to universalize. In this way, the risk-averse society is never risk-averse enough. Without the external understanding of the society's internal contradictions through the eyes of a dialectical Other, the society fails to adapt to reality and collapses.

The Last Supper (dir. Stacy Title, 1995) depicts a group of righteous graduate students who invite right-wing guests for dinner. They intend to murder these guests, serving them poisoned wine from a blue decanter – rather than a clear one, which contains the normal drink – unless they come to recant their political beliefs over the course of the meal.

After several successful killings, the students invite a famous conservative pundit to dinner. The pundit confuses the group with a range of moderate opinions that they have difficulty refuting. He even admits that the views he presents on television are for ratings and do not represent his true political positions.

Over the course of the dinner, the pundit pieces together clues that murders have taken place in this house. The students retreat to the kitchen to decide the pundit's fate, agreeing that his centrist views mean he should be spared. During this time, the pundit has swapped the poisoned wine from the blue decanter to the clear one and serves it to the students, raising a toast. As the film ends, the liberal students collapse on the floor and the conservative pundit speculates about a possible populist presidential bid.

Here, though the students profess liberal views, they are – as in the Master–Slave dialectic – conservative, acting in accordance with the Master's Discourse. They are unwilling to recognize the dialectical subjectivity of the Other, preferring to retain a frame of logic that sustains the status quo. This logic is unstable and contains within it the beginnings of their own demise.

Not only would an embrace of the contradictory subjectivity of the Other allow for the possibility of change that may transform the collective in surprising and emancipatory ways, but also to foreground the Lack that generates this universal contradiction is to challenge the logic of capitalist closure itself, whose symptoms at the level of culture the students might consciously condemn.

The students nullify the possibility of contingency within the Other by casting them as transcendentally belonging to a category of belief, unable to change and not marked by universal Lack. Like the contemporaneous "culture warrior" declaring their opponent to embody a "crypto-fascist" or "crypto-communist" position, the students engage in abstraction, claiming an a priori knowledge as to the destination of the chain of signifiers and the possible replication of the signifier "A" in another context. This utopian approach to language and logic necessitates an enemy whose presence explains away its impossibility. It resides within a paranoid-schizoid position, in Kleinian terms, demanding the destruction of the subjectivity of the Other and denying their possible conversion, undermining any opening toward the surprise and novelty of emancipatory politics altogether. It is a position contradicted in the film by the pundit's vacillating position. His adoption of political ideas as a televisual performance demonstrates his discernment or not-at-oneness with himself, a symptom of his marking by Lack and something that could be transformed in the right material and philosophical context.

The Irish comedian Dylan Moran suggests that war isn't conflict; it's the inability to do conflict.[13] If politics is the very act of engaging with the inevitably conflictual desires of the collective, then "culture war" is the end of politics. It pits groups who share higher-order interests against each other for the benefit of a capitalist class that resists change, even at the cost of the world's inexistence.

To be unrecognized in one's subjectivity is to experience a negation of one's humanity that is experienced as violent. The intransigence of the liberal students and their unwillingness to recognize the Other may be the very reason those they disparage have taken up their reactionary positions in the first place – in their subjective anxiety and material precariousness. The conservative nature of their politics affirms their subjective investment in the logic of capital, which alienates and exploits the collective and casts blame upon them for their suffering in the face of the impossible material conditions it creates.

The final scene of the film, in which the pundit sees himself leading a populist uprising, expresses the way in which this kind of revolt can be motivated by a libidinal *ressentiment* against the liberal Beautiful Soul, an action that is disastrous for the universal politics that would undermine the cultural phenomena that – consciously at least – the conservative students claim so fervently to stand against, as well as the political economy that generates the material conditions that foment reactive anger in the first place.

The Chain of Signifiers – *Un chien andalou*

Hegel's philosophy of contradiction anticipated the later linguistic developments in critical theory identifying the slippage between signifier and signified, insights that are also fundamental to the logic of psychoanalysis.

When Hegel writes in *The Phenomenology* that A does not equal A, he is describing the way in which the word "never" has a one-to-one relationship with the object it describes.

When we think of the word "apple," a world is conjured for the subject beyond a single image of an apple they might see in their mind's eye. "Apple" refers to health – "an apple a day keeps the doctor away"; it evokes desire – the forbidden fruit, or "the apple of one's eye"; it conjures religion – the Garden of Eden; it speaks of a great metropolis – the Big Apple; it refers to technology – the famous corporation – and to economic decline – the monopolistic rise of this corporation, and its failure to pay tax.

The slippage between signifier and signified is a well-known sticking point for translators. The universe evoked by one word in one language may open into greater expansiveness in another and its full meaning may be impossible to reproduce. "Space" might immediately refer in French to pastoral landscapes or – in Japanese – to the square footage of one's dwelling, but for an American or Russian, it might point to astronomy, innovation, conflict and national might. "Bread" for a French person might evoke revolution, culture and subsistence, but for an American it might evoke money ("dough").

The non-unification of signifiers across language is a symptom of the division of matter itself, splintering as it does into images of perception through subjectivity, and then through each subject's personal experience across place and time, this experience itself shaped by the further experience of individuals around them and by collective culture, both contemporary and historic.

The kaleidoscopic polyvalence of the junction between signifier and signified is why psychoanalysis takes so long – sometimes decades. Psychoanalysis works according to a chain of signifiers, a sense-making logic-by-juncture, which is potentially different for each analysand, just as meanings and words splinter off into infinite relationships across languages. This de-essentializes the role of language, breaking from the assumption that language refers to a pre-existing or essential reality outside of itself. In this sense, it is the opposite of the representational approach which looks to understand the hidden meaning in images because one image never ends with itself – it is always associated with another.

The time-investment necessary for the practice of psychoanalysis is why it is often the preserve of the rich, but it is also why its results are so elusive to the forces of commoditization and why ersatz psychoanalytic ideas take hold within culture, promising immediate access to the "hidden" truths about oneself, about the world and about – in some instances of film theory – the concealed meaning of a film or the inner workings of the mind of a director.

The length and inaccessibility of the psychoanalytic practice is why readily available "unconsciousness"-raising practices such as film might have political worth in terms of the philosophical transformation of wider society. What psychoanalysis might take considerable time and money to achieve, film – when understood in terms of the Analyst's Discourse – might offer as a collective "transformance"-art-istic experience, guiding its viewership to an emancipatory insight in small doses.

Un chien andalou is a 1929 film by Luis Buñuel, written by Buñuel and Salvador Dalí. It is a classic example of Buñuel's surrealism in that it breaks from linear plot and works with the fragmented chains of images that make his films so recognizable. In one sense, this would make it the antithesis of those films discussed in this book that achieve psychoanalytic impact on the viewer through well-constructed plot and guiding them to a point of revelation – potentially the Gaze of Lack – via affect and transference. However, when seen less as a celebration of anarchic fragmentation and more as an exploration of the metonymic approach of psychoanalysis, this kind of film can be seen as a version of putting the viewer through an episode of free association, like a dream. In this sense, it might radically make visible the infinite search for meaning in answer to perennial Lack.

Hiding in Plain Sight – *Storytelling*

In the *Encyclopedia of the Philosophical Sciences*, Hegel states, "'A cannot at the same time be A and not A.' – This maxim, instead of being a true law of thought, is nothing but a law of abstract understanding."[14] What he means here is that by denying that the signifier "A" can be at the same time "A" and "not A," the thinker is not adhering to the dialectical understanding of matter and signs ("Absolute Knowing"), but rather neutering the radical opening of contradiction in reality, in favor of binary, oppositional, ideological reasoning.

Though many industries are now using AI to produce initial drafts, later to be "brushed up" by humans, the inadequacy of programs such as Google Translate speaks to the dialectical knowledge required to work with the contradictions of language in its various forms in a way that the binary logic of machines cannot handle. When I was a French teacher, one of the most common tells that a student had used the "help" of Google Translate in their homework were phrases such as playing in an "allumette de foot" (a football match [that you might use to light a candle]) or the fact that there were "vingt-cinq maisons d'embarquement" at the school (boarding houses [as in boarding a plane]). These examples show the computer's necessary and inevitable impetus to force the signifier A to replicate as A in another context.

Computers cannot think because they are born only once, created as-they-are at the hands of human subjects. They are not born twice and are therefore not self-conscious. Computers process literally, not poetically or metonymically. They are divided insofar as matter is divided at the level of quantum oscillation, but they are not divided at the level of consciousness.

Against the digital attempt to reproduce A as A, language – born of Lack – cannot ever hit the nail of meaning on the head. Like a wet bar of soap that constantly slips from the grasp of those who attempt to handle it, language productively fails at direct communication, always pointing in a novel direction according to a connective logic. Like ions that form chains with more ions according to their lacking electrons, words latch onto more words according to the non-fulfillment of their role to signify a signified.

The failure of communication generates a surplus in language. Its failure generates poetry and art, just as subjectivity's universal formation-by-failure points toward a possible universalist, emancipatory politics.

Art's power over subjectivity resides in its ability to house contradiction within its structure and to operate on unconsciousness. What is perhaps unique about the artform of film is its ambition to totalize. Whilst structured storylines corral Lack within film toward a potentially productive point of revelation as to the true nature of desire, films that attempt to repress contradiction altogether are propagandistic. However, the very attempt to repress contradiction within the artform is exposed by it. The attempts sit ill with the viewer and are obvious. They may incite productive discussion since they reveal in relief the binary logic of ideology against the truly contradictory nature of life that art may more readily capture than oppositional abstraction.

Comedy, like art, is made possible by the contradictions present in language and logic and productively exposes them. Humor often relies on the presence of two conflictual truths within a signifier at the same time (for example, a child speaking like a wizened adult). Lacan comments[15] on humans' ability to manipulate contradiction via comedy and word play in reference to a famous joke from Freud about a couple of men who meet on a road in Poland. One man asks the other, "If you say you're going to Cracow, you want me to believe you're going to Lemberg. But I know that in fact you're going to Cracow. So why are you lying to me?"[16]

Here, Lacan shows that humans are able to hide truth not only in fiction, but also in non-fiction. This, he says, is one of the principal differences between animal consciousness and human subjectivity. He continues his analysis using the example of hunting. Animals, pursued by a hunter, leave tracks. Slier animals are able to conceal their tracks or leave decoys. It is up to the wily hunter to decipher these illusions. There is only one kind of "animal" that can leave true tracks that are intended to be read as false: human beings. Only humans are able to hide the truth in the truth. As Groucho Marx's joke goes – one that Žižek often recounts: "He might look like an idiot, sound like an idiot, but don't be fooled, he really is an idiot."[17]

Storytelling (dir. Todd Solondz, 2001) is a film divided into two halves: *Fiction* and *Nonfiction*. In *Fiction*, MFA student Vi writes the short story of an abusive sexual encounter with her Pulitzer Prize-winning instructor for a class crit. Vi's story provokes outrage amongst her fellow students. They call it outlandish, unbelievable, even though Vi found photographs in her professor's apartment that show the opposite is true – nearly all her course-mates have had sex with him. The students are outraged, therefore, not because the story is unbelievable, but precisely because it is. And Vi has put that truth in the wrong register: fiction.

Žižek recounts the story of a thief who left his factory every night with an empty wheelbarrow. Every night, the guards inspected the empty wheelbarrow and, never finding anything inside, waved him on, until they later came to understand that he had in fact been stealing wheelbarrows. Since ideological subjects are captured by a logic that truth is concealed from them, Vi would have done better to hide her truth in a register where no one would ever find it: the truth.

There is an impetus to understand psychoanalysis as a process that aligns with the satisfying logic of the detective story. Like the conspiracy theorist, the ideological subject gains satisfaction in the belief that the truth of their life is concealed from them. Whilst this mistake allows the analysand to libidinally invest in the "powers" of the analyst via transference, only to be let down later when they are revealed to possess no special knowledge, the political truth of psychoanalysis is that material reality is the limit of the subject's horizon. To think in terms of a concealed topography of subjectivity and matter is for the subject to hold themself hostage to a fantasy of an alternate world in which everything would be resolved for them, if only things were different. Instead, life is a calamity only made possible by a primary apocalypse whose contradictions are ongoing. By coming to terms with the contradictory nature of the world around them as it is, the subject can live more productively – less toxically – as long as they are alive, by working to transform a reality that is actually theirs, not an alternative universe that only exists via psychic abstraction.

Being, Becoming – *Babe*

Psychoanalysis is the philosophy of self-consciousness and is therefore a universal practice. Psychoanalysis charts the ways in which subjectivity – in a possibly infinite way for each individual – is not at one with itself. This non-at-oneness is called the unconscious.

Psychoanalysis developed as a theory and practice in response to the suffering experienced by subjects at a certain point of human civilizational development. Whilst different societal orders produced different modes of suffering – for example, the fear of the retribution of God in Hell for the subject's transgressions in feudalism – industrial capitalism produces a form of psychic disquiet that is so acute precisely because its antagonisms are so radically denied, it being the most modern form of societal development – and therefore the most adept at repressing its contradictions.

The main antagonism repressed by the market system is surplus value, which is predicated on the sacrifice of workers. This contradiction is obfuscated with cultural concessions and a puritanical focus on the ethics of "meritocracy," which – when they fail – are further papered over by ideological justifications that explain away these failures as contingent, rather than inherent to the structure of the market system as such.

Whilst capitalist ideology affirms particularity in terms of identity-as-commodity and the logic of ownership, psychoanalysis affirms universality (a traditionally "leftist" or emancipatory position) via its explication of the journey to subjectivity that follows the same pattern in all subjects – though explodes into infinity in its manifest form – and its revelation that no subject can overcome their Lack via the commodity.

The Master Signifier of capitalism (exemplified by "free," unfettered access to the market) is totalitarian in that it posits a false universality via the logic of exclusion (of those from whom surplus value is appropriated) and exception (for those who appropriate it). The symptoms of capitalism are manifested in response to its unbearable principal contradiction – the foundational "sinthome" of surplus value. The universality of psychoanalysis undercuts the false universal of the Master Signifier. All human subjects have something in common – nothing itself. The Master Signifier can never be universal and thus is an abstraction from the concrete "denaturedness" of universal subjectivity.

According to psychoanalysis, subjectivity is premised upon the signifier. Language, and therefore subjectivity, is formed through the impossibility of communication.

Humans are born with a potential to speak and think that is not yet actualized. For Hegel, at this point they are conscious, like other members of the animal kingdom – a status that may be likened to the Sartrean In-Itself.[18] Humans are distinguished from other animals via their second birth into language and subjectivity, a status that is For-Itself.

As compared to other animals, born with a greater physical readiness, humans are unindividuated at birth. Unlike the pony, for example, that can stand on its feet moments after birth and run, the human baby is born as a fetus, utterly dependent for many months on their primary caregiver as a result of their large skull and the small birth canal of the human adult, itself a result of the fact that we are bipedal.

The infant cries and laughs. The caregivers are lacking subjects who are unable to directly discern the meaning of their baby's communication.

Gradually, through frustration, the infant comes to speak. Speech is therefore a symptom of the contradiction of human biology, the Lack in the infant and the Lack in the parents.

Since the status of the pre-linguistic infant was Consciousness, the subject is forever endowed with a sense they have lost something substantive: an imagined oneness with their caregivers where their every need was met. This oneness is a fallacy in that the lacking parents were never able to faultlessly care for their child and the self-conscious child-as-divided-subject did not exist in its infant form. As for Adam and Eve for whom Eden became utopic only upon their expulsion from the garden, the pre-linguistic "oneness" of infancy is only transcendent insofar as it was lost.

This loss of an imagined oneness is subjective Lack. We are universally marked by it as long as we are alive. This Lack drives desire and makes life worth living. Capitalism exploits the fallacy that Lack is loss, offering an imagined access to the oneness via a commodity that could close it, but never can.

The second birth into language is that which opens self-consciousness within us and endows us with drive, rather than instinct. It also alienates us from the apparent oneness of matter.

The imagined totality of ego is cut through by the unconscious, which means – though we must invest in the stability of ego to navigate the world – we are never at one with ourselves. We are riven with contradictions. Suffering may occur when we attempt to overly rationalize these contradictions, instead of allowing them to dwell within us, all at once. The ongoing process of recognition through the eyes of the divided Other provides us with an egoic stability that the precarity of capitalism, and the commoditization of the Other, constantly threatens.

To be human is to be other to the material self; this otherness is the inevitable result of Lack in matter.

Babe (dir. Chris Noonan, 1995) is about a pig who is a sheepdog. According to psychoanalysis, Babe has traversed the second birth into language and therefore is a subject. He is a creature of language and thus marked by both Being and Becoming. In Being, he is a pig. But Hoggett, the farmer, has identified a capacity in him to herd other animals and, by proving his utility, he will not be eaten for dinner. In Becoming, Babe is a sheepdog. He learns the signifier required to herd sheep (Baa Ram Ewe) and transforms into a prize-winning dog. Language brings the subject beyond biological necessity and permits them to inhabit multiple identities at once, syllogistically.

Radical Sex – *The Piano Teacher*

The term "little death" in French ("la petite mort") refers to the nothingness to which the subject is exposed after orgasm. "Mort" refers to the death in the subject's desire after the completion of the act. It can be traumatic because it points the subject toward the nothingness at the heart of something that is imagined to be transcendent, as well as their emergence from the contradiction in matter as such. Fantasy and foreplay are the necessary crutches which allow the subject to enjoy the sexual act as gratifying rather than traumatic. Rape is so violent precisely because of the psychic harm it entails when the subject is not involved in the sexual act on the level of fantasy.

Sex is given primacy in psychoanalysis not because it is the underlying cause of everything else, but rather because it presents a critical moment in the subject's structure by desire – a moment of pure confrontation with Lack that can, in the right philosophical context, point them toward a better understanding of their subjectivity and its place within the world, orienting them toward insights that might lead them to live in more constructive and liberatory ways, both as individuals and in community.

Sexual fantasy forms for the infant as a response to the question of what their primary caregiver wants of them. It is an attempt to stabilize the Lack in the subjectivity of the Other and, in this way, is a defense against Lack. Since it arises at such a young age, sexual fantasy is inevitably base, irrational and scatalogical.

Historically, conservative societies managed the necessary impurity in sex in its infantile logic via the scapegoat mechanism. These modes of social organization condemned certain forms of desiring as impure in order to envisage heterosexual modes of desire as pure by contrast. In reality, because of the fundamental illogic of all sexuality and because of the way it is structured via the "impurity" in contradiction that it attempts to manage, all sexuality has Lack in common. This is what is meant by theorists who claim that all sexuality is queer.

The historical conservative punished and excluded the "queer" subject via a false logic of purity in order to manage the impurity that was present within their own sexuality. Whilst neo-liberal politics has commoditized the promise of queerness by particularizing sexuality, according to a product-based logic of identity categories with which the subject is encouraged to identify via a logic of exception rather than universality, what is radical in queer theory is the universality of disorder in sex, in subjectivity and in our universe. There is no resolution to the queerness of our universe. The political act of queerness is to reside in its universal contradiction and not to overcome it via Death Drive, scapegoating and commoditization.

When wrapped up in its fantasy, when guided to orgasm by the act of foreplay and intercourse (or even browsing a dating app), the subject can suffer the death of their desire in small doses. Likewise, film – especially narrative-driven film – can draw the subject by their desire and place them in the position of the orgasm enjoyer in order to confront them – in a way that they can manage – with the nature of their desire and offer them a terrain of possible philosophical and political insight.

In the moment of their orgasm, the subject can be understood as the perfect capitalist consumer, moving toward what they believe to be their desire's completion like a good addict in the throes of an imagined ecstatic hit. Then, at the moment of orgasm, the subject is returned to itself, confronting the contradictory nature of their desire and its impossibility, like a user who feels both the relief and disaster of another hit.

The structure of film, which guides the viewer by desire and anticipation through a riven story that charts the possible fulfillment or non-fulfillment of a protagonist, which focuses the viewer's attention through sumptuous color, sound and music, acts upon the subject like foreplay upon the subject engaged in sex.

An ideological reading of sex and film would have it that the most valued moment is that of the final release of orgasm or the final revelation of the fate of the protagonist. This logic is that of the pleasure principle, focusing on the possible orgasmic ecstasy offered in the completion of a goal or the attainment of a product. Instead, it could be politically and philosophically fruitful to place import both on the death in the viewer's desire following the resolution of the plot – exposing the death in desire that cannot be assuaged via the commodity – and on the fantasy that is the necessary obstacle facilitating a tolerance of the death in desire, which can be productively enjoyed according to a logic of True Infinity, reducing the suffering of the subject and the resultant *ressentiment* the subject feels when they imagine pleasure has been contingently stolen from them, which can have negative, oppositional effects.

The Piano Teacher (dir. Michael Haneke, 2001) expresses how traumatic the end of desire can be, against a process of foreplay and excitation that appears as the obstacle to the act, but is in fact the site of enjoyment. Fantasy protects the subject from the trauma of the death in desire; orgasm protects the subject from the trauma of the Lack in the Other's fantasy.

In the film, sexually disturbed pianist Erika is engaged in an affair with her talented student Walter. After Erika confesses the contours of her fantasy in a letter to Walter, he is disgusted, the fantasy revealing the dark, scatological, repulsive desires of the piano teacher. When Walter finally agrees to enact Erika's demands to be attacked and raped by him, Erika has achieved her sexual fantasy and is confronted by the horror of its hollowness. In despair, she stabs herself in the chest.

The Universalism of Psychoanalysis – *Alien*

In the history of film theory, *Alien* (dir. Ridley Scott, 1979) has been misunderstood at times as containing a singularly feminist message, rather than – potentially – a Marxist one. Film's subjectivity is manifest in the vacillation of its apparent philosophical impetus according to the context in which we view it, reflecting to us the contours of our moment and its capitalist desire. A feminist reading may have been most pertinent at the time of the film's release when women had been long excluded from aspects of public life; at a time when gender-based progress narratives have been weaponized to mystify the workings of capital (for example, "girl boss feminism"), a materialist critique may be most fruitful and may expose how particularisms can stymie, in the longer term, the psychoanalytic contribution to emancipatory politics.

An influential contemporaneous interpretation of *Alien* used psychoanalytic language to show that the film illustrated the prevalence of misogyny within culture by revealing how the female reproductive system is associated with monstrosity ("the monstrous feminine").[19] Here, the facehugger that attaches itself to a crew member's face exemplifies the horror of the vagina.

Misogyny results from an excess hatred for femininity that emerges from the subject's anger at their deprivation of the imagined oneness offered by the breast that was taken from them by their mother and the ambivalence (joy, disgust, resentment) they feel at the notion of ever having been born. It relies on the "female-ness" of the caregiver only insofar as it is ideological (that it is an unconscious mechanism by which the subject rationalizes their Lack as an exception). Whilst sexuation exists according to gendered difference, there is no transcendent essence to "female-ness" or "male-ness" not only because a woman can so readily be or become a man, but because there is no transcendent essence in existence in the universe, other than that which is experienced as such by the subject in excess, because of their marking by Lack.

The recognition of the existence of misogyny is vital, but it is not the end of the analytic process. It is a cultural symptom that is a starting place for a material analysis that may gradually overcome it. Its universal nature (stemming from the birth process through which all subjects pass) speaks to the political potential of an analytic reading of the phenomenon as symptom.

Whilst psychoanalysis would expose the subject to the material foundations of the symptom in order to create the libidinal and philosophical conditions for a potential material transformation of the psychic economy that generates it in the first place (by rationalizing Lack as a contingent, non-universal loss that can be overcome), some components of psychoanalytic theory have come to maintain their analyses at the level of the cultural. To do so is to remain within abstraction, solidifying the Real at the level of the Imaginary instead of elevating it to the level of the Symbolic, which is the very definition – for Lacan – of the process of analysis.

Oppositional theory sustains the identification of the symptom as its end point and avoids the dialectical work of tarrying with Lack and all its implications, explaining away the symptom as an indication of the transcendent purity/impurity of given groups or of poor subjective behavior on the part of a specific group that can simply be resolved by conscious, disciplinary solutions. Since these solutions are abstracted from the dialectical Real that underpins our world, they sustain its repression, with new symptoms returning with renewed intensity.

Further, the problem-solution logic of these interpretations is readily commoditized by the market. In film, this can manifest in various ways. A film might consciously display moral rectitude and become a commodity that promises to assuage a Lack in the viewer by disciplining them. The (im)pure identity of the maker – abstracted from the material reality that generated it – might endow the film with an imagined transcendence via a wisdom that the audience can appropriate according to an Orientalist logic. Conscious moral purity within the film's narrative structure can be appropriated as cultural capital by the beneficiaries of surplus value who can perform a familiarity with the "correct" knowledge proffered by the film, which itself acts as a veil to conceal the immoral and illogical workings of the system that benefits them. These factors are antithetical to the universalist, political structure of the film mechanism and work to repress it.

The University Discourse uses already existing cultural and political biases to understand the manifest content of the film and is therefore conservative. An approach that pertains to the Analyst's Discourse positions the viewer in relation to a productive encounter with the infinite potentiality of the Lack within the film itself, which may offer a conversion experience through the destabilization of these biases – film not just as symptom, but as process.

In the canonical film theory essay "Visual Pleasure and Narrative Cinema,"[20] it is argued that feminists should "fight the unconscious" as it appears in films marked by the so-called "male gaze." In this reading, films made within the context of patriarchal capitalism display "unconscious" evidence of being so. In psychoanalytic theory, however, there is no substantive unconscious and therefore no unconscious-as-entity to fight. The unconscious is a fissure present in reality at all times, a residue of the ego's aim for totality as a mechanism by which the self-conscious subject, as a child, comes to navigate the world. The symptomatology of the film does not end with "patriarchy" itself, but rather with the eternal contradictions of subjectivity and the universe which must be continually productively and politically tarried with, lest the subject collapses into reactionary thinking, a historical example of which is patriarchy itself.

Taking the insight that *Alien* exposes misogyny within the culture to its psychoanalytic conclusion, we might come to a stronger political interpretation. Misogyny is not just a feature of the gender wars, but rather a toxic artifact of subjective life, one that capitalism sustains by denying subjectivity's contradictions and one that can be challenged by raising the trauma of the Real to the universal Symbolic Order, a process that itself undermines the logic of capitalism.

The arrival of all subjects from Lack creates a latent anxiety in them, regardless of gender, relative to the birth process. The attraction–repulsion toward and against the vaginal symbolism in *Alien*, and the fact that viewers of every gender can identify with the horrors on show, reveals the universal subject's anger at their deprivation of the imagined oneness of Being. The hatred here is not directed to women because they are women, but because they gave birth. In a different scientific order, one that some have argued we are heading toward, whoever gives birth

– male, female or other – may come to face the same unconscious hatred, which itself, through philosophy and psychoanalysis, would have to be tarried with and the trauma of the Real of it neutered by its digestion into the Symbolic.

Further, whilst it has been argued that the alien creatures in the film code female in their aesthetic proximity to human genitals, it cannot be denied that the xenomorph has characteristics that appear "male" (the large head, the phallus-shaped alien fetus that bursts out of a crew mate's chest). Whilst there is anxiety for all subjects in relation to the Lack from which they emanate (the vagina), there is also anxiety related to the phallus – both its possession and its absence, as exemplified in Little Hans' fear of horses in Freud's famous case.

The universal Lack within the viewer and the Lack within Ripley-as-subject allows transference to occur between them and for subjects of all genders to identify with her. Part of the universal power of the film's horror resides in its depiction of the Lack within the monstrous Other – the mystery of the dialectic of subjectivity, necessary for recognition to occur, but terrifying for the subject who can never anticipate how the Other might act or what they desire of them.

As many theorists have pointed out, *Alien* expresses drive, a feature of all human subjectivity – an insatiable, eternal force that pays no attention to the "pleasure principle" (the reassuring notion that humans are motivated by utility, rather than their own destruction). The alien is more like themselves as humans than the crew members aboard *Nostromo* would like to admit: zombie-like, unrelenting, it destroys all around it in the attempt to survive, even against its own well-being. The alien is a mirror to the capitalist subject who would maintain a non-dialectic understanding of their reality, even at the cost of their life.

Perhaps the most terrifying message of *Alien*, however, is that – two centuries after Hegel, one and a half after Marx, one after Freud and a half-century after Lacan – human society has still not come to terms with the political import of Absolute Knowing, the emancipatory potential of an embrace of universal Lack. The religiosity of commodity fetishism is so powerful that it remains across centuries and may never be undone. Still slaves to surplus value, the crew believes at the start of the film that they have earned their money and are on their way home. Instead, they are forced by the corporation to risk their lives once again or forfeit the fruit of the sacrifice already made.

Romantic Exception – *Bridget Jones's Diary*

Pride and Prejudice is sometimes read as a proto-Marxist novel in that it foregrounds the material conditions of the Bennett sisters in the context of securing their future via marriage. Whilst the novel is certainly more materialist than most cultural products today, the ideological closure offered by the story – that Elizabeth is exempted from precariousness by marrying into wealth and, at the same time, finds her perfect match – has meant that its story structure has been readily commoditized and has become recognizable in perhaps the most ideological of narrative forms: the rom-com. *Bridget Jones's Diary* (dir. Sharon Maguire, 2001) is one of the most successful examples of this genre and is a near calque of *Pride and Prejudice* onto the life of a young woman in contemporary London.

Here, the subject imagines that the solution to their economic constraint is not to work collectively to overcome capitalism, but to invest in exception: like the lottery winner, they could be absolved of material constraints by a wealthy person who not only is themself sufficiently Marxist to understand contemporary economics and to conceive of the person of desire outside of capitalist ideology (i.e., they are not desirable because of what they offer, they are to be loved "just the way they are"), but also is able to offer the subject a life beyond the antagonisms of capitalism within it. The rom-com depoliticizes the subject, transforming the politics of Love into the commodity form of romance. This is perhaps why it is a genre most enjoyed by the subject at the precise moment they experience the market system's downsides (for example, after a break-up) and need to be soothed. By offering an ideological solution, the depressed subject is able to mourn their losses and re-knit the chain of signifiers via a renewed fantasy. But it is a temporary fix; by re-investing in capitalist fantasy, they will inevitably be let down again.

The rom-com became particularly prevalent in the nineties and noughties when economic conditions allowed for the cultural supremacy of mid-budget films. It has been argued that the contingent prevalence of the rom-com during the childhood and adolescence of millennials has been disastrous for their adult love lives, having led them to ideologically invest in an exception that can never arrive, rather than accepting the dialectical reality of love: that it is to invest in the Lack of the Other. Tragically, the more precarious their material conditions, the more driven they may be to invest in this fantasy.

It is not only the millennial who can invest in the 30-something Bridget and be exploited by the ideological currents of the film in which she appears. A 70-year-old male viewer may identify with Bridget and her desire to be the capitalist exception. Whilst the potential identity characteristics of the human subject are infinite because of the prism of Lack, capitalist desire follows a singular, unconscious logic – the assuaging of the gap of Lack in fulfillment.

Just as the subject is endowed with desires that are not theirs, but become theirs, during their entrance from consciousness into language via the play of recognition and misrecognition with the subjectivities of their lacking parents, the lacking, self-conscious adult can readily adopt desires that are not originally their own, but become them, via mimetic desire.

The fact that even a well-intentioned environmentalist or a carefully conscious anti-capitalist may find themselves, through a narrative like that of *Bridget Jones*, desiring along ideological lines shows capitalist desire is mimetic and that it operates unconsciously. Conversely, the fact that the subject is so easily shaped and directed by the process of mimetic desire speaks to an emancipatory potentiality in film. The artform that so readily captures the subject's libido could be consciously directed toward a productive understanding and relationship with the object of desire through an investment in a narrative form that gradually lets the subject down. Further, as an object of study, the collective enjoyment of ideological film informs us of the contours of our capitalist desire, reminding us – with political effect, if considered assiduously – how and what we do in fact desire, despite our conscious claims to the contrary. In this sense, our collective desire "speaks through" the ideological film and what is spoken – as in the process of psychoanalysis – can be analyzed.

Capitalist Death Drive – *Brazil*

The slogan of the dating app "Hinge" provides an interesting example of the contradiction within capitalism that ideology is constantly at pains to deny. The app's slogan claims that it is "designed to be deleted." It asserts that the app is so successful at matching its users that its purpose is to self-destruct.

As a profit-seeking enterprise, the opposite is true. The profits for its shareholders rely on its failure to match its users, not its success. In order to sustain revenue, the app relies on daters who continue to date, not those who succeed in finding a partner. The market system foregrounds its successes, but they are exceptions that prove the rule. Whilst Steinbeck stated that "everyone was a temporarily embarrassed capitalist,"[21] today we might claim that – in our epoch of platform capitalism – everyone is a temporarily frustrated Hinge dater, just as they may be a temporarily frustrated SoundCloud rapper, viral YouTuber or TikTok meme creator.

A common argument from capitalism's supporters is that it is the most logical, reasonable and productive form of organizing society because it is so utilitarian. Capitalism's detractors also often use this argument – that it is an overall negative to human flourishing precisely because it is too utilitarian and doesn't match the complex nature of human life, reducing everything in the world to objects to be exchanged. Perhaps neither of these logics fully captures its toxicity, which resides not in its tendency to be utilitarian, but rather in its necessarily destructive quality, which always creates and offers a problem that must consequently be "solved."

Death Drive is the attempt by the subject to eradicate the dialectic by returning to a oneness that is not even possible in death (the subject returns to the earth as minerals, which are themselves oscillating at the quantum level, and becomes again part of a human subject via their consumption of food). The subject protects themself from their contradictory status by driving toward objects and phenomena that they believe will quell their Lack. Since they can never reach the oneness of fulfillment because it cannot exist in material reality, the subject must perpetually put distance between themself and their object of imagined fulfillment, which will inevitably let them down, in order to sustain its magic.

Brazil (dir. Terry Gilliam, 1985) depicts the Death Drive in capitalism – how the system exerts itself over the collective via its failure. Those involved in the bureaucratic edifice depicted in the film fail to do anything, whilst striving to appear rushed and busy. One of the system's outlaws is handyman Harry Tuttle, who comes to the aid of individuals who have broken devices in their homes. By fixing these devices, he is the enemy of the state whose own handypeople must keep the machinery of the system broken in order to justify their own existence.

The very inciting incident of the narrative occurs when a squished insect fudges Tuttle's arrest warrant in a teleprinter, resulting in a misunderstanding that the wanted criminal is Buttle. What is important here is not that the totalitarian hyper-bureaucracy is undermined by a mere fly, but rather that it is sustained by it, echoed by the structure of the narrative itself, which is incited by the mistake.

Capitalism necessarily creates bad products that do not meet the needs of the collective. Under the regime of corporate oligopoly, seemingly more like the techno-bureaucracy of *Brazil* every day, it is nearly impossible to create work outside of the auspices of capitalist Death Drive. Today, good work, and good films, are an exception, even a miracle. Great films are produced, but are often unrecognized, explained away, shielded from the view of the public lest they expose the failures of the center. Occasionally, though – through the miracle of contradiction – they do appear and they can be embraced.

Nonetheless, like Tuttle, most filmmakers and artists must often work bandit-like, with the scraps of an ever more totalizing system, in the knowledge their work might never be watched.

Gaze of Mastery, Gaze of Lack – *Vertigo*

In Lacanian terms, Gaze is a residue that appears in excess between interfacing subjects or subjects and objects. It confronts the subject with the constitutive Lack at the core of being.

Gaze challenges the ideological notion that sight is unmediated. Of the five senses, sight is often misunderstood as the most objective ("I saw it with my very eyes!"; "it was in plain sight") or totalizing (we can be said to have "20/20 vision" or a clarity of "hindsight" and "foresight"), as compared to taste, for example, the very word conveying discernment ("I have a taste for cherries, not chocolate") or touch ("it felt wrong").

In his *Four Fundamental Concepts of Psychoanalysis,* Lacan says of Gaze that "what is profoundly unsatisfying, and always missing, is that you never look at me from the place from which I see you."[22] Since subjects are divided, looking always involves a process of infinitely reciprocal recognition and misrecognition and brings with it a reminder of the "armor of an alienating identity"[23] with which the subject is endowed during the mirror stage, in the face of which they always feel inadequate.

The divided parent necessarily misrecognizes their child in two principal ways. First, the child is sufficiently frustrated by the failure of the lacking parent that they must come to speak and therefore think. Second, the lacking parent reinforces the child's sense of self by lending their look to the process of visual reinforcement that occurs during the mirror stage. Gaze is the resultant residue between parent and child. The parent's process of seeing – lacking, therefore discerning – affirms their child's vision of themself as a bounded being in their reflected image. This is the armor of an alienating identity that allows the subject to navigate the world, but it endows them with an uneasy sense of inadequacy and non-totality in the face of an imagined Ideal Ego, a Cartesian subject who appeared for them in the mirror and whose mind and body seem to be connected.

"Male gaze" identifies with the "mistake" of masculine sexuation in that it expresses the male artist's subjectivity as a powerful entity, objectifying the female subject who becomes a helpless object beneath the command of their phallic camera. Whilst the idea cut against the trends of misogyny within filmmaking culture at the time of its conception and may in fact implicitly critique the "mistake" of the Impostor that the Lacanian Gaze exposes, the way the concept has been understood – or misunderstood – in mainstream culture arrests the radicality of Lacan's universalist concept and lends weight to the notion that there is an intransigent, "hidden" totality to male perception via the use of psychoanalytic language. Here, there is no male or female essence to Gaze since Gaze concerns the identity of the looking subject as much as that of the Other (the subject/object who returns the look and exposes the viewer's necessary subjective division). A particularist understanding of Gaze as one of mastery aligns with the Bad Infinity of capitalism, which suggests both that there is a singular subject who is undivided (uncastrated – having stolen an amassed jouissance for themself) and that the Other can ever not be implicated in the processes of perception and desire.

This commoditized understanding runs contrary to the impetus of Lacan's revolutionary ideas of universal alterity and the public nature of subjectivity and desire, including those that marked early dynamics in queer theory, which show that all sexuality is queer because it forms around Lack and that there is no subjectivity without division. The "male gaze" came to have a near-unprecedented impact upon the language and ethos of film studies and filmmaking, within the institution and the cultural mainstream, perhaps because the way it was understood made no challenge to the underlying ideology of capitalism that engenders economic inequality and instability, which intensify and maintain forms of oppression such as misogyny, where a group or class must be subjugated for the extraction of surplus value. The progressive nature of the critique even came to operate as an unconscious fetish to deny the dynamic of this underlying ideology within film practice and the wider economy.

In Hitchcock's *Vertigo* (1958), Scottie – an ex-detective who has retired from police work because he suffers from vertigo – is hired by an old friend, Gavin, to follow his wife, Madeleine. Gavin claims that Madeleine is acting strangely and he believes she is being haunted by her great-grandmother Carlotta, who died by suicide. Gavin fears a similar fate will befall Madeleine. In reality, Gavin has already murdered his wife and has hired another woman, Judy, to portray her. Judy lures Scottie to a tall clock tower from which she appears to fall. Too afraid to stop her, Scottie sees only a body on the ground, which does not belong to Judy, but rather to the original Madeleine. In this way, Gavin exploits Scottie's phobia to cover up the murder of his wife.

According to "Visual Pleasure and Narrative Cinema," *Vertigo* expresses a misogynistic "male gaze" in that "the look is central to the plot, oscillating between voyeurism and fetishistic fascination." Scottie, as a policeman, is "exemplary of the symbolic order and the law." He has "the power to subject another person to the will sadistically or the gaze voyeuristically" and turns this "onto the woman as object of both."[24] While it may be the case that Scottie is a misogynistic man, that the film was produced within a misogynistic culture and that Hitchcock, like male directors of his time, subjectivized men as male characters and objectivized women as passive facilitators of plot, this critique is not aligned with a Lacanian approach, but rather perhaps with Foucauldian critiques of manifest systems of power.[25] In fact, by positing that the misogyny present in the film exists because of the totality of male subjectivity, rather than its Lack, it falls into the oppositional, capitalist logic that Lacan aimed to undermine via this theory. Lacanian Gaze exposes the Lack in all subjective structures, predicts the political potential of hysteria in all and claims that cultural symptoms such as misogyny are a result of the attempt to deny the denaturedness of all human subjectivity upon an economic terrain that must promise oneness in alterity in order to extract profit. For Lacan, all Gaze is Gaze-of-Lack. The possibility of a Gaze-of-Power is an ideological illusion.

Indeed, a Lacanian analysis of the film's most iconic scene would yield a universalist insight, showing that Scottie is equally as lacking as

Madeleine, that the patriarchal power that he has does not offer what it promises, subjectivizing them both and leading to the logical conclusion that misogyny is a symptom of the attempt to deny universal Lack, rather than embrace it, and that a society based on its unconscious recognition might facilitate the undermining of the subjugation of one group by another – be they male or female or of a given class or ethnic group.

In this scene, Scottie follows Madeleine/Judy to an art gallery and finds her gazing at a portrait that appears to be a near replica of her and that turns out to depict Carlotta. The "male gaze" invites us to read this moment as an example of the image of the woman already existing in the eye of the man, constructed by an active masculine power, which disempowers the woman and forces her to respond to this demand. Madeleine/Judy looks at the picture, but she will never live up to the image in Scottie's eyes – the female is the lacking subject in an apparently patriarchal world. Madeleine/Judy is small and appears lower in the picture, she sits meekly in a position comparable to that of Carlotta as she submits to the framing of the screen, which itself mirrors the perspective of a domineering male director.

This moment, however, depicts the universal Lack in Gaze in numerous ways. The resemblance/mis-resemblance of Madeleine/Judy with Carlotta exposes how the universal subject can never live up to their Ideal Ego, a factor that haunts subjectivity and makes it possible. Here, Scottie is confronted – and through him, the viewer (male, female or other) – with incomplete reciprocity. We see that the Other is not their Ideal Ego and is divided. The division in the object of sight (even when apparently passive) returns the Gaze of Lack upon the viewer, since this division subjectivizes the object according to Hegel's quantum notion of substance being as subject.[26] For example, the chignon worn by Madeleine/Judy is terrifying, looking more like the flared nostrils of a stallion than the one worn by Carlotta in the painting. The roses in Carlotta's hands are not the symbol of romantic unity, but of difference – "there is no sexual relationship"[27] – as they sit not in Madeleine/Judy's hands, but next to her on the bench.

What we see here is not Scottie in the position of "master" and Madeleine as "slave" but the dialectical and intersubjective relationship between them, as well as its traumatic reminder of the universal Lack at the core of two subjects in a moment of misrecognition. The universal Gaze sits between subjects and reminds them that this Lack is what they both are, against the comforting illusion that the male is uncastrated, a master who has amassed all the jouissance in the world, the reappropriation of which can be commoditized via a logic of the promise of oneness-in-identity.

The Mysteries of the Egyptians Were Mysteries to the Egyptians Themselves – *Caché*

Caché (dir. Michael Haneke, 2005) is an anti-colonial film insofar as it challenges the Orientalist logic of oneness in alterity. It shows that there is no exception in subjectivity, that the ego is master in the house of neither the Westerner nor the colonized subject – all Becoming is marked by universal Lack. A universal politics based on this insight may generate a future where the exploitation and subjugation of the Other ceases to continue in the excessive ways that it has marked capitalist society because there is no promise to be commoditized in that Other.

Caché depicts a bourgeois-bohemian literary critic in Paris (Georges) who begins to receive packages containing video-tapes of his house. It is unclear from whom these packages come and whose perspective they depict. Georges then receives cards depicting a childlike drawing of a man having his throat cut and, later, another video that depicts a working-class suburb.

In the first instance, the undefined Gaze of the videos evokes an unease in Georges, exposing his own Lack, so easily forgotten in his milieu as an upper-middle-class television host – he is directly confronted with the anxiety of Gaze ("What does the Other want of me?"). The ambiguous signifiers and the sense he is being watched stir a guilt in him as he begins to conceive of the sender: Majid, a boy, now man, of his own age whom his parents adopted following the death of his parents during the 1961 Paris massacre of Algerians, drowned by the police in the Seine.

Aesthetically, the film borrows motifs from the work of Camus. Whilst in the work of the absurdist, the Arab is barely subjectivized and is conceived of as a threat to the pied-noirs who know nothing of the Other's desires, and is haunted by the mystery of their Das Ding (the dimension of desire that it is impossible to imagine), Haneke's work goes further by subjectivizing the orphan Majid, whose desires are shown to be ambiguous even to himself. In a final interaction with Georges, a tape recording of which is sent to him, Majid denies any knowledge at all of the packages and slits his own throat.

Whilst conservative identity politics sustains the logic of colonization by consciously elevating and unconsciously debasing the subjectivity of the Other by casting them as "wise," "all-knowing" or "noble" and thus of a transcendentally alternate subjective status to the Westerner, thereby preserving the possibility of oneness in totality on which the commodity logic of capitalism relies, emancipatory politics posits a shared Lack that can never be defeated in life or death. This insight inspires a universal politics of collectivity rather than exception and challenges the enemy-making dialectic of utopianism upon which exclusion, exploitation and subjugation are predicated.

Recognition and Identification – *Ingrid Goes West*

The screen medium of social platforms has come to dominate collective life. Particularly since the pandemic, interfacing between dialectical subjects in the public sphere has been replaced by commoditized interactions that take place via a screen. This has had destabilizing effects for the subject, who – unrecognized – will inevitably come to invest further in an imagined absolution offered by capitalist logic, which itself facilitates the greater extraction of surplus value from the subject and their greater, second-order alienation.

Whilst everything that was once sacred has been profaned by market forces – for example, many young people can no longer afford to have children and neoliberal ideology has defeated the reactionary dynamics within institutions such as marriage and religion, but also the reassurance they once offered – the inability for social media to offer recognition to the subject has redoubled the absence of the latter in a society that no longer provides roles.

The Other of social media is a commoditized object who is portrayed as whole and complete. Materially, Tiktoks and Instagram posts evoke the totality of the star-on-screen as witnessed during the Hollywood Golden Age, but do not – like film at its best – expose the star's Lack. Tweets have the aesthetic authority of black typeface against white, synonymous with the published word. This has endowed the Other of social media with the appearance of being more authoritative than they are. As Dolar has pointed out,[28] this is a phenomenon that has had disintegrative effects on the social collective where we witness – forever, once published – the opinions of others, rumor and gossip (once relegated to the private sphere) with the traumatic veneer of officialdom, leading to a distrust of the Other, to self-policing and to a libidinal investment in cancellation when it seems like the only recognition available in the privatized public sphere.

Whilst the dialectical complexity of film allows for the viewer to be let down in their transferential relationship with the subject portrayed on screen, social media provides a non-dialectical, non-relationship with the Other. On corporatized platforms, where even the "like" is a commodity, an individual's page is not only the locus of their personal brand, but also the site of labor extraction. Whilst the ethos of philanthropic capitalism, a derivative of corporate oligopoly, drives subjects to simultaneously display their successes as well as all that is stacked against them, both phenomena – even the latter, "more authentic" one – are commoditized. The Other, therefore, appears whole and complete even in their non-completeness. Lack becomes loss via commodity logic.

Recognition through the Gaze of the divided Other – only possible because of the discernment they offer because they are divided – is what generates the ego in childhood and facilitates the navigation of public life that would otherwise be experienced as traumatic. The process of recognition is ongoing throughout the subject's life and vital. Since the Other of social media appears undivided, they cannot offer the subject the recognition via discernment that would usually occur in the intersubjective encounter.

The addictive nature of social media confirms that no intersubjective recognition is taking place there. The subject curates their brand via their social media page and attempts to reality-test their identity via the reception of "likes" and "comments." When no recognition occurs, the subject comes back for more. Any attempt the user makes to assuage their Lack through Instagram ultimately feeds it. Finding no recognition on these platforms, the subject's mode of enjoyment in relating to them becomes one of the *ressentiment* of "annoy-ment," the painful pleasure of envious voyeurism, laughter at the Other's earnestness or irritation at the logic of the "humblebrag" which pervades the self-commoditization into which the subject of social media is forced according to the contradictory logic of philanthropic capitalism.

Ingrid Goes West (dir. Matt Spicer, 2017) is the story of a down-and-out millennial who invests in the Instagram posts of a successful influencer from Venice, California (Taylor). Ingrid distracts herself from her own material conditions by imagining that she and Taylor could be friends. She blows her inheritance on a short-lived trip to Los Angeles to stalk her prospective bestie.

Over the course of the film, through the inter-subjective productivity of the real-life encounter, Ingrid comes to understand that Taylor is as miserable as she is, that she is insecure, that Taylor's apparently perfect boyfriend is in fact a pathetic, untalented leech, although it takes Ingrid failing at an overdose to truly reach rock bottom and confront her life.

Whilst the film offers an exception of closure in that Ingrid broadcasts this overdose via Snapchat and receives recognition for doing so in the form of her post going viral, she comes at length to understand that she has repressed an acknowledgment of her dialectical reality and the possibility of finding joy in ordinary unhappiness according to her own desires, having invested so heavily in a fantasy that was not hers. According to the logic of the living flower, Ingrid is able to build a new life and create new love in the world as it is, not as she fantasizes it might be.

"Jouir à cause des entraves" – *The Dreamers*

The Dreamers (2003) by Bernardo Bertolucci expresses how film can shape desire, even on the level of eroticism. In '68, three students – American Matthew, and Parisian twins Théo and Isabelle – imitate the films they watch at the Cinémathèque Française and play sexual games according to the dynamics they see on screen, conceiving of this pursuit as intrinsically political. Evoking Genet's *The Balcony*,[29] the political action of the film in fact takes place outside their window. Whilst the notion that "the personal is political" may be well known to them, it seems that the students have misunderstood its principal tenet – that the personal is political insofar as each individual is connected to the universal via their Lack. It is perhaps clearer, therefore, to say that the *inter*personal, or the intersubjective, is political; the individual sexual escapades of bourgeois students certainly does not constitute productive political activism in and of itself.

Whilst, in the film, certainly more activism is taking place in the streets of Paris than between the students' bedsheets, it has been recognized by many that the student protests of '68 took a non-emancipatory turn in their misunderstanding of the politics of desire in which they were invested. Rather than conceiving of desire as universal – and therefore non-capitalistic – the promise of transcendence in desire re-particularized the universal phenomenon, resulting in the expansion and solidification of capitalism via the ethos of the protests, even into realms that were previously conceived of as outside its sphere of influence. The sexual revolution lost its emancipatory potential when it became invested in a utopian (non-divided) logic, leading to the commoditization of sex and relationships and the exploitation of sexual desire in the advertising of products.

The utopian turn in the politics of '68 can be viewed in the slogan that commanded the subject to "jouir sans entraves" (enjoy without limits). Politically and psychoanalytically, this is a logical impossibility: it is precisely limitation that generates desire.

Capitalism relies on the illusion that there is both a transcendence on offer in getting what we want and that obstacles to the object of desire are contingent and eradicable, rather than necessary to sustain enjoyment. Whilst the melancholic experiences a loss in their desire by attaining the longed-for object and experiencing its impotence, the depressive is unable to enjoy the loss of the object that it feels spiritually connected to, but materially separate from. Whilst utopian logic focuses on the possibility of fulfillment, emancipatory logic undermines the capitalist Bad Infinity by encouraging the subject to enjoy the creative possibility of their Lack as such.

In the film, the three students have huge amounts of sex but remain unfulfilled. They fall into a sexual stupor. Isabelle attempts to restimulate desire by enacting loss – a murder suicide, which itself is abruptly interrupted, and the students' desire restimulated, by the intrusion of the external, political world when a brick is thrown through their window.

It is for this reason that Lacan warned the students of '68, "ce à quoi vous aspirez comme révolutionnaires, c'est à un maître. Vous l'aurez"[30] (What you are looking for as revolutionaries is a master. You will have one). From this perspective, the conscious revolution of the students was not a political one, but rather one that solidified capitalist desire and that mystified – but sustained – the Master Signifier of capitalism. What the students misunderstood about desire was that one cannot enjoy without constraint. Enjoyment is only possible because of it. What is political in psychoanalysis is the transformation of desire in relation to the obstacle, the enjoyment of the obstacle toward a Good Infinity when the subject understands there can be no end to their desire and there is therefore no need to desperately scapegoat, subjugate and exploit to sustain it.

Who, or Where, Is the Emancipatory Subject? – *Pig*

Many of the trends in contemporary arthouse and experimental cinema have regarded themselves as progressive in their move to fragment grand narrative structures and splinter the film form, seeing form and narrative itself as restrictive and repressive. These movements have cast heavily structured and plotted narratives as conservative. But the highly structured nature of narrative film could, in fact, be seen as the apotheosis of emancipatory cinema and precisely that which may challenge a conservative mindset, not only because it is popular and libidinally compelling, but because it offers a mechanism that unconsciously transforms desire.

André Bazin criticized the tendency of cinema to seek or simulate fantasy, arguing that cinema is political insofar as it is realistic.[31] In the sixties, Noël Burch built on Bazin's work,[32] arguing for a new, emancipatory "cinema of the future" that would break from the limitations of the kinds of narrative structures favored by mainstream cinema – viewed, by him, as ideological and politically dangerous – into a progressive, fragmentary, experimental form that would be the ally of class consciousness and liberation. But this anarchistic approach has not yet yielded a liberatory class consciousness it aspired to and, in fact, has contributed to the greater mystification of capitalism precisely because it promised liberation without confronting material conditions and was an ethos readily commoditized by the market, whilst simultaneously offering a cathartic Imaginary that confidently affirmed progress and change.

Film is not political in its representational qualities, but in its psychoanalytic characteristics. Unless art transforms libido, it remains within the capitalist register, often redoubling the toxicity of the system via mystification.

Audre Lorde posited that "the master's tools will never dismantle the master's house."[33] Whilst it could be claimed that the "traditional" narrative form of plotted cinema represented the "master's tools" during the Golden Age of early twentieth-century Hollywood and during the supremacy of American popular culture in later decades, given the changes to the economic and cultural order via the rise of the state-sustained corporate oligopoly, today's master's tools may in fact be very different and may pertain not to the riven narrative form that characterized traditional cinema, but rather to the aesthetic (a)politics that has come to decorate studio films and to the anarchistic, non-materialist approach that has come to dominate the "independent" sphere. Across both spaces, the identity of the maker has often been granted supremacy over the artful content of the work – a logic of solipsism and commodification that has outstripped the political potential of a focus on the universal viewing experience of the public. Many critics, perhaps fearful of losing their footing in a precarious landscape, read works not according to the artistic qualities of their manifest content, but according to the work's ideological adherence to culturally accepted points of view or the identity of those who made it. Thus, much of film culture has missed the political possibility of the encounter with the novelty of Lack in film. At a time of immense economic precarity – and with the ever-present threat of the trauma of finally accepting the failures of the system in which we are all so deeply, unconsciously invested – a repression of the productive Lack in film as artform acts as a soothing fetish to protect ourselves from the truth of our reality, to which Lack (in film's Gaze, in the unexpected non-unity of artistic output and identity, in the challenge to comforting ideologies) would orient us.

Similar to the philanthropic drive amongst robber barons during early twentieth-century monopoly capitalism, the immoral workings of corporate oligopoly have demanded an appeal to moralism to both mystify its functioning and to drive a wedge between different population groups who would have greater sway if they collaborated according to the universal logic of Lack and recognized their shared interest. Impecunious graduates are able to sustain a fantasy relationship to the tragedy of their impoverishment precisely by their debt-inducing neoliberal education by adhering to the moral logic of the University Discourse that sets them apart, consciously at least, from the proletariat – to which, monetarily, they in fact have become aligned. The University Discourse may claim to know in advance the direction of political change, but it is in fact an aesthetic, apolitical and utopian logic, as evidenced in its disciplinary dynamic and its impulse to fetishize the Other according to the conservative promise of Orientalism.

Whilst the University Discourse confidently pre-codes the contours of a revolution that may never come, the Analyst's Discourse remains open to the surprise of potentiality within the political space. Whilst well-meaning activists may nominate a given group with transcendent promise, absolving themselves of political responsibility in the process, past revolutions have shown that transformation can occur in the most unexpected of places.

In revolutionary Russia, for example, in nineteenth-century France and during the Arab Spring, certain tipping points toward the potential of change came about when the soldiers turned their weapons away from the people and toward those in power. It was precisely the master's tools that offered an opening toward political change, so much so that political theorist Benjamin Studebaker has argued that perhaps the most terrifying and reactionary component of our political future is the replacing of soldiers and police with non-subjective robots.[34] Whilst training desensitizes soldiers and police to the repressive violence they enact on behalf of capital, there is always a possibility of transformation in the dialectical human subject, whose division by the unconscious leaves them open to hysteric change, to see the human in the Other, to question the illogic of the system they defend and to understand the righteousness of siding with the collective. Robotic creatures cannot do this. Armed with weapons and programmed to kill, there is absolutely no potential for subjective change and therefore no threat to systems of power.

Pig (dir. Michael Sarnoski, 2021) is a film that exploits contours of the traditional film form, resulting in a range of emancipatory insights. It is a political film dressed up as a traditional, Hollywood caper, exploiting both the genre expectations of the thriller form and the casting of Nicolas Cage, who metonymically – as a signifier – evokes a particular universe as an action figure.

The viewer invests in the traditional narrative form here, following a reclusive truffle hunter whose pig is stolen by criminals, only to be surprised by the contrast to their expectations offered by the universal insight of the film's revelation. Structurally, the quest appears to be an oppositional one: Rob, played by Cage, is motivated to retrieve an object on which his income seems to rely or to enact redemptive violence on those who stole it from him. Instead, in each encounter with the Other (in this case, his former colleagues from the high-end restaurant business that he has renounced in favor of an impoverished life), Rob exposes the contradiction and insincerity of their choices via recognition. For example, his own ex-prep chef has given up on his dream of running a pub in favor of a trendy *haute cuisine* restaurant and confronts, through Rob's eyes, the tragedy of his decision.

Later, instead of taking revenge on the mob boss (Darius) who orchestrated the stealing of his pig, Rob cooks a special meal for him, the same as the last one Darius and his wife had enjoyed at Rob's restaurant before her death. In sharing the meal, both Rob and Darius are subjectively transformed.

In this encounter, they each witness the Lack in the Other, recognizing the grief they have both experienced in losing their wives and they are able to mourn via the consolation of the experience of the other.

For Rob, who has abstracted himself from public life after the death of his own wife and forgone the possibility of conversion via the subjectivization of the Other through his quietism, the journey into the world has exposed the contradictions and limitations of his own approach. Having mourned her, he is able to re-subjectivize her and finally enjoy the sound of her voice via a recording she left of herself singing *I'm on Fire* by Bruce Springsteen.

Distinctly, but just as importantly, the viewer – who has come to invest in the transcendent quality of the pig according to a logic of commodity satisfaction – is let down in their cinematic investment, exposed to its Lack, when they discover that the pig has been dead throughout the entire film, killed even before Rob embarked on his quest by the incompetent addicts employed to kidnap it, and already made into bacon. Whilst using the Hollywood cinematic structure, all parties – characters and viewers – come, through the film, to embrace the fundamental Lack in life – which, taken to its final logic, is life's end – precisely because the film's traditional form inspires a libidinal investment that leads all parties to Lack and exposes to them in relief, in an analogous dynamic to psychoanalysis, where the analysand's "misguided" investment in the analyst's non-division is precisely that which allows them to be confronted with their own Lack.

Whilst we can look to history and employ philosophical reasoning to explore the patterns in our repressive system to imagine the future contours of possible political change, *Pig* reminds us that we may not know in advance where the emancipatory subject will be found or what form a revolution might concretely take. By predicting these things, or particularizing their location, we may sustain the libidinal economy that entraps us, conferring an individual, group or dynamic with transcendent potential and transforming the promise they hold into a commodity that can be bought and sold and therefore neutered of its radicality.

Traversing the Fantasy – *Phantom Thread*

Traversing the fantasy is the process of recognizing that the subject themself is the source of the sublime quality of their fantasy and that this sublimity is only made possible by the unconscious oscillation between the hope of achieving the object of desire and the reality of its impotence. The subject enjoys the undermining of the attainment of the object of their desire and may unconsciously participate in its sabotage. The subject's desire is sustained by their perpetual circling – and non-attainment – of the lost object.

This is the universal structure of subjectivity, but the dynamics of this structure, as well as the form the object of desire takes, differ in potentially infinite ways, a phenomenon that makes manifest both the operation of the material world on the subject's form of desire and the non-fixity of subjectivity at the point of its emergence from Lack.

The subject's fundamental fantasy is a decision that they do not make; it is one that is made for them via the contingent experiences of their early years. Fantasy is a means by which the infant has rationalized their place in the universe relative to the contradictory desires of those around them – in particular, the uncanny, destabilizing desire of their primary caregiver, whose wants for them the child can only guess. This structuring of the infant's subjectivity via fantasy condemns them to play out their (mis)understanding of the desire of the Other for the rest of their life.

Since this fantasy structure assists the subject in managing their own Lack and protects them from the trauma of witnessing their own self-division, the objects around which the subject's fantasies are oriented take on a transcendent power. This power is illusory. If the subject attains the object of desire, they fall into melancholy, confronted by the object's blunt impotence. If they find themselves too far from it, they fall into depression, and must engage in a process of mourning during which they stitch together the puncture in the chain of signifiers provoked by this loss, reorienting themself toward the object again according to a new logic.

Once the subject is able to accept and digest the structuring of their desire by Lack, to bring the Real of their desire to consciousness, they are able to traverse their fantasy. Here, the problem of desire is not resolved, but, rather, enjoyed. The sublime of desire is understood as an "immanent transcendence" that emerges from Lack, which must continue to be undermined to be sustained.

Thus, in the traversing of fantasy, the negation of desire is negated. The failure of desire is transformed into a generative possibility. The subject is therefore now able to "fail better" since their investment in the power of their object is no longer transcendent but material. Since the subject is the origin of the sublime in their own fantasy, to traverse it is to de-otherize jouissance. The subject acknowledges that no Other has stolen their jouissance; it was with the subject all along, unrecognized and enjoyed.

Whilst, ideologically, love might be represented by terms referring to a lover like "a soulmate" or "twin flame," expressing two perfectly matching sides of the same whole that can be unified in oneness, love involves the imperfect play of Lack and fantasy. In love, for Lacan, the subject receives something they do not want in their partner – the end of a fantasy that the "one" will utterly fulfill them – via something they do not have – the Lack in their subjectivity and the structure of their own fantasy. To love, then, is to traverse the fantasy. The lovers find in each other not a fulfillment of their fantasy but a Lack that scuppers the perfect attainment of "object a" and makes possible an infinite investment in that which the other does not have.

Phantom Thread (dir. P. T. Anderson, 2017) depicts how sado-masochism can be an embodiment of love. Famed fashion designer and avowed bachelor Reynolds Woodcock falls for waitress Alma Elson. She becomes his model and lover, though there is immense tension in their relationship. Reynolds is obsessive and rigid; Alma is equally stubborn and refuses to be controlled. The couple, each party as intransigent as the other, cannot find equilibrium in love. Alma tries to win over Reynolds with displays of affection; Reynolds lambasts any disruption to his meticulous routine.

Neither Alma nor Reynolds realizes that this conflictual pattern sustains their love by undermining the fantasy that each other is the perfect match. Each gains enjoyment from the imaginary ideal that the other could perfectly assuage their subjective Lack and fit perfectly into their lifestyle and routine. By sabotaging their relationship, they luxuriate in the fantasy of a perfect fit and do not realize that it is the imperfection of the other – that each seeks to dominate the other and have them yield to their own desire – that sustains that very desire.

Alma resolves to take revenge upon Reynolds, poisoning him with wild mushrooms. Alma nurses him back to health. They reconcile and marry, but, after their honeymoon, they fall back into their conflictual patterns. A client suggests to Reynolds that his work might be losing its edge. Reynolds confides in her that Alma's presence is a distraction and that he is considering divorce.

Alma overhears this conversation and poisons Reynolds again, this time with a wild mushroom omelet. Reynolds now willingly eats the dish. Alma tells him that she wants to make him sick and dependent upon her. By bringing their conflictual dynamic to consciousness, Reynolds and Alma begin to enjoy the jouissance of their inevitably impossible relationship. By corralling the conflict of domination and submission to the play of poisoning and nursing back to health, a dynamic they experienced as unpleasant becomes enjoyable. They identify with their drives, with the undermining of their own desire, and no longer suffer – in their wider lives – as a result of them.

Not only is a film such as *Phantom Thread* an object lesson in traversing the fantasy, but the structure of film itself can encourage this process by using plot to corral the desire of the protagonist to a point of revelation, exposing the viewer to the inevitable Lack in their desire and the primacy of the process of plot/fantasy in terms of the subject's enjoyment.

Only a Christian Can Be an Atheist – *The Wizard of Oz*

Perversely, consumer capitalism not only directs the subject's libido toward commoditized objects that they are told to desire through advertising, but also tells the subject that they can be fulfilled in their desire by a specific object at all.

Today, this lie is often repressed via fetishistic disavowal. The atheistic subject of contemporary life may very well be aware that there is no promise in fulfillment via the commodity, but, as Octave Mannoni explains, the subject operates on a logic of: "I know very well, but all the same . . ."[35] The fact, for example, that studies have shown branded medication to work better than non-branded medication on the symptoms of illness, despite being composed of precisely the same chemical ingredients, speaks to the continued way in which belief in the commodity's mystical powers operates upon the contemporary subject's mind and body, despite the confident logic of atheism having pervaded much of public and private life.

Capitalist companies may express conscious knowledge of the impotence of the ideology of promise, but mere lip service in this regard does nothing to transform the functioning of their company's bottom line. For example, in the recent Mattel-funded film *Barbie*, many of its characters offer critiques of the company's own products and practices, but Mattel continues to rely on the premise of the ideology of promise – that the subject can be fulfilled in the purchasing of one of their commodities – to sustain its business model.

It is as if non-belief is precisely that which sustains belief within the contemporary capitalist world. As the subject approaches its trauma in recognizing their unresolvable constitution by Lack, they radically turn back away from it at the last moment by avowing knowledge of the way capitalism functions in order to disavow the traumatic truth of the Real of their desire.

Over the history of theology, many thinkers – from Ernst Bloch to Heidegger, Paul Tillich, Simone Weil, Thomas Altizer, William Hamilton, Don Cuppitt and Žižek – have made this claim in relation to Christianity. For Bloch, "The best thing about religion is that it makes for heretics . . . Only an atheist can be a good Christian; only a Christian can be a good atheist."[36] It is only in giving oneself over fully to the promise of fulfillment in belief that one can confront the impotence of that belief in reality and the ultimate truth of the division of the nature of the universe – that we are less than nothing.

Throughout the history of psychoanalysis, misguided criticisms have been leveled at it for functioning in a patriarchal, absolutist way, promising a solution to the subject's lacking desire. For the critic, psychoanalysis presents a knowledgeable figure of singular authority who holds command over their analysand, who often lies vulnerable and exposed on the couch. The "patriarchal" analyst is said to tell the analysand how they desire and offer a solution to the problems of that desire.

Of course, the opposite is true. The ultimate insight of psychoanalysis is that there is no all-knowing Big Other offering a solution to the conundrum of the subject's contradictory desire, and the job of the analyst is to work with the analysand to gradually come to terms with this reality and incorporate this insight within the workings of their life.

There is an aspect of the well-worn critique, however, that does carry weight. The critic of the analyst's authority misunderstands the divided nature of the analyst themself, but their delusion in their belief is one with which the analyst would hope the analysand arrives at the start of their analysis.

In order to enact transference upon the analyst, the analysand must believe in the analyst's capacity to "cure" them. This is what Lacan refers to in his comment that "les non-dupes errent"[37] (the non-duped are mistaken). This is play upon "le nom du père" (the name of the father), a function that is missing for the psychotic subject who is, initially at least, unable to enact transference upon the figure of authority. In this case, the analyst must position themself differently toward the analysand in order to emphasize the role of the "father," rather than undermine it.

For the non-psychotic subject, in order for the psychoanalytic relationship to play out between analysand and analyst – for the analysand to successfully project their desire upon the analyst – the analysand must, at first, be duped by the analyst's authority.

The over-investment of the analysand in the knowledge of the analyst is like that of the Christian believer in the power of God. It is only because the analysand has invested in the promise of the analyst's knowledge that the gradual disabusing of this illusion can take place and that the analysand is capable of confronting the Lack in their desire. The play between two lacking subjectivities – that of the analyst and that of the analysand via transference and countertransference – creates a subjective experience in surplus and the conditions for subjective transformation. This generative experience is not itself transcendent, beyond contradiction. Rather, it is manifest from Lack and could not be generated any other way.

Film has a similar power to generate something "immanently transcendent" in the subject as a result of the transferential relationship between the viewer and the screen. The viewer, lacking in their desire, invests in the desire of the protagonist as the analysand invests in the knowledge of the analyst. They experience excitation at the prospect that the protagonist will be fulfilled in their desire, and that so – in the position of the spectator – might they.

Furthermore, like Freud's Fort-Da game, the plotted film plays on the expectations of the viewer, involving them psychically in a repetitious process that piques their desire. Films in Hollywood are bought and sold by genre. Scripts are pitched according to the ways they play on and subvert expectation (an agent selling *The Shallows* might claim, "It's *Jaws* meets *Castaway*!"; *Inception* might be sold as *The Matrix* meets *Memento*) and attract a paying audience via offering anticipation in what they know and the thrill of what they might not.

Through the Fort-Da game, Freud recognized the way the child derives pleasure from the repetitive action of making an object disappear then reappear as a means of coping with the anxiety caused by the absence of their primary caregiver. The game also exposes the importance of repetition in both the psychic development of the subject and the ways they invest themself libidinally in the world around them.

The effects of investing the viewer's libido in the point of revelation are two-fold. First, film has the capacity to consciously disabuse the viewer of the existential power of the promise in fulfillment by raising their expectation and exposing the emptiness in their desire in relief via revelation. This is the logic of the ripping of the temple curtain in the Jewish tradition. Second, the viewer is able to cope with the trauma of the loss of fantasy via the excitation of the plotted form as the child who manages the loss of the breast in the Fort-Da game. By pleasurably disabusing the subject of their investment in ideology, film can help orient the viewer to a political relationship with reality and the Other.

The Wizard of Oz (dir. Victor Fleming, 1939) provides a famous example of the temple curtain ripping at its point of revelation. Dorothy and her colleagues discover that the Wizard is not the all-knowing deity they hope for, one who can solve their problems in an instant, but rather a man behind a curtain who offers them the insight that they already possess all the knowledge they require. The power of this insight is only made possible by the transferential relationship the characters have with the Wizard and the subsequent quest on which they embark, the active process of which exposes them to the insights that they latterly come to understand through their encounter with him. They are shown by the Wizard what they already know and would otherwise not have understood unless they embarked on their journey with the motivation to discover knowledge they believed was concealed from them.

Although *The Wizard of Oz* is a conscious example of the exposure of the audience toward the Lack in desire and the Lack in the Big Other via the nature of its plot, all film structured around a story has the capacity to offer the viewer a "small death" in their desire. Whether the character with whom the viewer identifies is fulfilled or not, the orgasmic release in the answering of the primary question posed by the plot confronts the viewer with the end of their desire. This release may be dissatisfying, if it accords with the pattern of the impossible promise so prevalent in capitalism, or productive, if the question is answered in such a way that it opens the subject toward the impossibility of their desire as such.

Film, because of its capacity to mobilize and undermine desire, has the capability of functioning like psychoanalysis upon the subject in this way to confront them with the Lack in their desire and – ultimately – the Lack in the universe as such.

Outopia – *Children of Men*

Just as Lack generates speech, thought and subjectivity, as non-completion is that which generates and sustains desire and as sex offers pleasure in the obstacles that lead up to the "little death" of desire in orgasm, the chaosmos of the universe – in all its depth dimensions, difficulties, darkness – offers the productive grounds from which an emancipatory political collective can emerge.

Though common cultural assumptions might have it that psychoanalysis turns its interest inwardly toward the desire of the individual subject, it is political insofar as it transcends particularism and leads the subject toward their universal status as a lacking subject. Further, it points to the social nature of desire. Desire is only possible within a social network. There is no transcendent desire that exists before the emergence of subjectivity, but rather subjectivity is the vessel of desire and the subjectivity of the Other generates the Lack within us that inspires our own desire and teaches us, foundationally, how to desire.

Lyotard is often associated with postmodernism but is better understood as a critic of it. He attended Lacan's lectures in the mid-sixties and subsequently coined the term "libidinal economy"[38] to describe the material economic system of capitalism in which we desire – and which is driven by desire. Because of the social nature of desire, we cannot "opt out" of the libidinal collective and, in fact, by consciously choosing to act as superior, "ethical" subjects beyond the libidinal fray, we may end up suppressing the contradictions of capitalism all the more, leading to greater suffering in the return of this repression.

While a long history of certain well-meaning "political" projects that accord with the logic of the Beautiful Soul shows an aspiration to be removed from the problem of existence, dreaming of utopian alternatives or cleansing oneself of complicity in a corrupt system and projecting moral insufficiency onto the Other, for psychoanalysis – as for Lyotard – the only way out is to recognize the libidinal structure of the system, comprised as it is of every subject's interpersonally evolved desire, and transform it.

Just as there is no possibility of the consciously pure ethical consumer extinguishing their capitalist libido without politico-social transformation, the philosophical insight into the structure of the subject's capitalist desire does not extinguish their ability to desire and to enjoy. In other words, by subscribing to an anti-capitalist agenda, we do not prevent ourselves from desiring within the parameters of capitalist desire. Likewise, critiquing or making visible the structure of desire – as is being delineated here – does little to change it. It does, however, offer the subject the chance to think about creating practices – for instance in art or perhaps, in particular, in film – which might be oriented toward a change in our relationship not to our own individual desires, as so much discussion is oriented, but to our social and collective interpersonal role as desiring subjects, even – or perhaps most especially – on an unconscious level.

One key feature of a practice oriented toward changing the desire of the subject would be its immediacy: it would not be rooted in utopian promises for the future.

Utopian visions of society are always dystopian in practice. Psychoanalytically speaking, the toxicity of the fascist's vision of utopian purity is that it is never total enough because it cannot embrace Lack. The totalitarian transforms the Lack that is foundational to the universe and human life into contingent loss.

The formation of an enemy, necessary to cast as a possibility a world without loss, creates and maintains the conditions for oppression and alienation of the collective and of the oppressed class in particular, in order to sustain income for the few, generated – under capitalism – by surplus value. On a societal level, the transformation of capitalist desire through the logic of psychoanalysis is not to reduce the utopia to its dystopian opposite for dystopia is precisely what is present within the logic of utopia as its returned repressed – as Ian Parker has posited,[39] Stalinist realism accords with the Bad Infinity of capitalist realism and is just as right-wing. Instead, the analyzed desire acts according to an alternative logic – one that might be termed "outopian."

The circular infinity of an outopian society might accord with Hegel's logic of the True Infinite, as an alternative to the Bad Infinity of capitalism. Here, the toxic excitation of drive is assuaged, but not extinguished. The subject is able to enjoy the productive consequences of their Lack in sustainable ways, not by being presented with a promise of a future, but by being allowed to embrace the contradictions of desire in the present moment. In this sense, Hegel, Marx and Freud all opposed utopianism. Utopianism, like capitalism, believes in the possibility of an undivided subject to come, whereas the only possible route to change comes from rejecting this ideological myth, embracing the emancipatory present where action toward change can materially take place. This logic not only holds philosophically, but practically: the urgency of our present moment demands a transformation that takes place within it.

Žižek borrows the term "possible worlds"[40] from analytic philosophy to describe the ways in which subjects can be caught up in alternate universes where a utopia could exist, even when they have accepted the death of perfection in their own life. Though these worlds are not possible, they can hold sway over the subject, distracting them from the emancipatory power of the enjoyment they might experience in their life within the contradictory present.

The Christian apocalypticist may embody this libidinal dynamic. Unable to digest the complex, and imperfect, nature of the world as it is, they imagine their experience is contingently difficult – not because of the material conditions their politics may or may not sustain, but because they happen to be living within the end times. Instead of transforming their society through collective political action, the apocalypticist turns their attention to a possible world where life could be better at the hands of a superior being whose whims they can appease, or if others believed in the way that they did.

Progressivism is at its most progressive when it rejects an ideological retroactivity that explicates history as a gradual, if stilted, process of improvement toward the present. This fetishistic approach can often compensate for poor contemporary economic conditions by focusing on the moral perfectionism of developing cultural attitudes. It is at its best when it turns away from a reality to come in favor of the direct moment, in all its contradictory possibility, embracing a universal politics that does not employ the non-progressive as a contingent obstacle who casts the fantasy of a perfect society in relief, but works with them in the understanding that the site of anti-capitalist politics is within the contradiction of the present and that the embrace of that contradiction may be the only means by which society can transform its collective libido from the reactionary logic of Bad Infinity toward an emancipatory one in True Infinity.

Children of Men (dir. Alfonso Cuarón, 2006) depicts a post-apocalyptic Britain where humans have ceased to reproduce due to the unlivable conditions that capitalism has produced. The government uses military force to defend its borders from immigrants who continue to travel to the country as one of the remaining states with a semblance of functioning government. In this context, a group of underground activists travel with a young immigrant woman, the first person to be pregnant in a decade, to a boat off the south coast called *Tomorrow*.

The dystopian society depicted in the film has been made so by capitalist utopianism. The promise of future profit has killed both the present and the future – as exemplified in the death of birth. There is literally no future for this totalitarian state, save for the pregnant immigrant. As the activists flee the country, Tomorrow only exists in the uncertain waters of the open ocean.

Political Film – *Two Days, One Night*

In *Two Days, One Night* (2014, dir. Dardenne brothers), a young woman overcomes depression via an encounter with the collective that allows her to digest and symbolize the Real of her despair. By witnessing the Lack in the Other and experiencing the recognition it can provide her, she is able, gradually, to confront reality as it is, not as she hoped it would be, and is able to embrace the Lack she psychically attempted to keep at a distance, manifested in her depression.

The film's structure is political and accords with the logic of Marx's living flower. This structure may offer a metaphor for the universal potential of film as such.

Sandra works in a Belgian solar-panel factory and has taken time off because of her mental illness. Her boss has proposed that her workmates share her salary since they have been able to manage her workload in her absence and it makes no difference to productivity if she is dismissed. There will be a vote on Monday to finalize the decision. Over the course of the weekend, Sandra approaches each of these workmates in a final attempt to convince them to vote for her return.

She has been bed-bound, but news of the decision is so painful that it is a catalyst for an existential shift in her reality. An Event, it offers the possibility of conversion in relation to the conditions of her life, but it is only through a confrontation with the collective that she is able to bear the weight of her loss and carry it.

In depression, the subject experiences a too-much-ness. A loss is felt as so great that the meaning of the subject's life has been broken. There is a rupture in the chain of signifiers and there is an invasion of the Real upon the subject. There is no space to desire anything else but the object that has been lost – in this case, Sandra's social role and her livelihood.

The process of encountering her colleagues allows Sandra to begin to knit together the broken chain. She is able to exit the horror of her subjective experience into a reality that indeed generated the horror, but that is more bearable once it has been symbolized and that must be tarried with in order to be transformed.

Although the vote does not pass in her favor, the intersubjective encounter with each of her colleagues allows for a process of recognition to occur. The very fact each colleague has the ability to choose one way or the other shows them also to be a dialectical subject, constituted by Lack. The stories they share of their own difficulties affirm not only that each subject is marked by Lack, but that they dwell together within an unproductive, inhuman economic order, the bringing to consciousness of which may lead to political transformation.

Sandra's contingent crisis allows her to confront and embrace this universal Lack. Not only is she buoyed by her own strength of will to confront her former employer, she is refolded into the collective by transforming her desire from a logic of exception (that a material event can assuage her suffering, which is constitutive) to an embrace of reality in all its grit, grime and tragedy. In this way, Sandra has been politicized.

Whilst utopian logic keeps the subject fixated on a future that will never come, the politicized subject is able to take action in the present, knowing that life exists here and now and that change can only occur in the infinite potential of this ever-unfolding moment.

Film can guide the subject, like Sandra, to a confrontation with the Lack in their desire, the Lack in the collective of subjectivity and the inadequacy of the economy we invest in to satisfy and sustain us.

Conclusion: Fail Again, Fail Better

Language Never Hits the Nail on the Head

In contrast to communication, which – when functioning properly – always means what it says, language involves an inherent misunderstanding. The reason for this lies in the way that language refers to a Master Signifier. This is a signifier that generates meaning, but which cannot itself be captured by meaning. Words such as God, Freedom, Justice and Love can act in this way: words that generate unending discourse, yet cannot be adequately captured by that discourse.

Anselm defined the word "God" as that which names something beyond naming.[1] Unlike communication, language is always "missing" something, which means that it can never be a closed system. In Derridean terms, we can say that language operates with an "undeconstructable" core that is a type of eternal absence that generates the very discourse that it evades.

Thus, the words of this book are doomed to fail in their attempt to capture that elusive quality in film that makes it so compelling and therefore so productive. The greatest aspiration I can have for them is that they generate more words and more discussion or that they inspire film work that may engage with psychoanalytic ideas in all their openness, mystery and contradiction, beyond the ways in which they have been conceived within the neoliberal ideology of identity, difference and closure.

Film as Theology

Human subjects are spoken into existence. We are overwritten by language that always fails and by desire that can never be fulfilled. In our impossible relationship with meaning and with fulfillment, drives are created, which – whilst endowing life with the depth-dimension that makes it livable – can cause us to act against our best interest in the religious hope that we can transcend our condition. Psychoanalysis and the Analyst's Discourse are therefore our much needed allies. But even aspects of psychoanalysis can be perverted by promises of fulfillment, of essence in the chaos of identity and in the nullification of Lack in the self and the Other, which undermine its very emancipatory power. This is particularly true when material conditions become so unbearable that we are drawn to ideological solutions that soothe us from the reality of our moment, precisely when it would be most fruitful to confront it.

Film, with psychoanalysis, may offer a cultural and political practice that operates on the collective unconscious and reorients us toward the infinite possibility of Lack, in place of the collective theological practices that existed under different forms of societal organization and which – when stripped of their repressive or utopian promises – allowed for the subject to live more practically, less toxically, dwelling within the mystery of the world.

A Privileged Artform

Film is the unique medium where Lack can alight. Whilst capitalism harnesses the specific ways humans attempt to overcome Lack, film can expose the viewer to it. In this way, it may act upon the analysand as the analyst in the process of psychoanalysis, which – at its best – confronts the subject with, and allows them to digest, the Lack in their subjectivity and the Lack in the world that generates them.

Film's capacity to perform this function is the result of many of its material factors. In addition to the unconscious operation of the film over the subject, a consideration of these factors via an analytic approach, as well as the manifest content of a given film, may also yield a philosophical and political potentiality for the collective.

The Re-emancipation of Public Life

Philosophy is tarrying with the contradictions of the universe. Politics is tarrying with the contradictory desires of distinct members within a group. Art is art insofar as it houses and exposes contradiction. Contradiction cannot be commoditized insofar as it cannot offer absolution from Lack, which is the precise reason we are most shielded from contradiction within capitalism – a tragedy given that an orientation toward it could transform the way we live in the world. Capitalism is an exploitation of the religious tendency in subjectivity – the drive to seek oneness in oblivion – and it offers none of the critique of this impulse that the best of confessional religion provides. It has encroached into nearly every crevice of modern life, perhaps most especially into the intersubjective relationship, to the extent that it has undermined itself and appears to be disintegrating and reformulating.

Capitalism may be collapsing into its new manifestation. The morbid symptoms of its crisis could confront us with the nature of our world and subjectivity and lead us, via collective politics, to a novel future. The greater repression of its contradictions could lead us away from the possibility of a future altogether. As in the society depicted in *Children of Men*, the Death Drive of capital could sacrifice our tomorrow in eking out the last possible element of profit from us today.

Under the pervasive constraints of oppositional capitalist ideology, even philosophy, politics and art have become disfigured as commodities. "Politics" has become an oppositional war of all against all that sustains the promise of utopia behind the contingent enemy of the Other whose vision of the world does not accord with our own. Much philosophy has come to accord with the University Discourse under the regime of the neoliberal institution where, instead of speaking and thinking freely, one must neuter one's insights in favor of a set of oppositional ideas that aesthetically accord with the history of thought, but in fact sustain the extraction of surplus value and the generation of scapegoats around whom the non-dialectical society rationalizes its own purity as it collapses.

Whilst film and art have long been commoditized to their detriment, the very structure of film, the way it operates on the subject's desire and unconscious, the way it houses contradiction and exposes its own repression of it, may offer the collective a mechanism by which to re-emancipate public life.

Whilst decades of theory and critique have exposed the toxicity of capitalism to the capitalist subject, it persists. Film, like psychoanalysis, may offer an alternative approach in its capacity to work against capitalist ideology via its work on unconsciousness.

Film is a technology that was first created only a few generations ago. Its power – mechanistic, in terms of affect and, most importantly, in terms of fantasy – has been glimpsed by makers and audiences, but often eclipsed by the oppositional logic of capitalist Bad Infinity. A collectivist medium, one that is widespread and popular, it speaks to our desire, our desire speaks through it and our desire is revealed to us by it. It is an artform that works with human unconsciousness and reflects it back to us. With the right approach, we may transform our relationship to the artform, libidinally and therefore politically and philosophically, which may yield for the collective an emancipatory present and future that we so desperately need.

Notes

Introduction: The Analyst's Discourse

1 Sigmund Freud, "'Wild' Analysis," *The Revised Standard Edition of the Complete Psychological Works of Sigmund Freud*, Volume XI, trans. James Strachey (London: Rowman and Littlefield, 2024), p. 217.

2 Julia Kristeva, *Hatred and Forgiveness*, trans. Jeanine Herman (New York: Columbia University Press, 2010), p. 194.

3 Alain Badiou, "Cinema as a Democratic Emblem," trans. Alex Ling and Aurélien Mondon, *Parrhesia* 6 (2009), p. 4.

4 Slavoj Žižek, *Less than Nothing: Hegel and the Shadow of Dialectical Materialism* (London: Verso, 2013).

5 Karl Marx, "Grundrisse: Foundations of the Critique of Political Economy," www.marxists.org/archive/marx/works/1857/grundrisse/ch15.htm.

6 Jacques Lacan, *Seminar XXIII: The Sinthome*, ed.

Jacques-Alain Miller, trans. A. R. Price (Cambridge: Polity, 2016).

7 Sophie Fiennes, dir., *The Pervert's Guide to Cinema* (2006).

8 Jacques Lacan, *Seminar XX: Encore*, ed. Jacques-Alain Miller, trans. Bruce Fink (New York: W. W. Norton, 2000).

9 Jacques Lacan, *Le séminaire. Livre V: Les formations de l'inconscient (1957–58)*, ed. Jacques-Alain Miller (Paris: Seuil, 1998), pp. 466–7.

10 Todd McGowan, "The Gaze in Cinema," YouTube, uploaded by Todd McGowan, March 28, 2020, https://www.youtube.com/watch?v=-ukJTaTgyQ4.

11 Friedrich Nietzsche, "Aphorism 108, Book III, The Gay Science," available at http://nietzsche.holtof.com/reader/friedrich-nietzsche/the-gay-science/aphorism-108-quote_6e7c2d49f.html.

12 Karl Marx, "Introduction, Critique of Hegel's Philosophy of Right," available at www.marxists.org/archive/marx/works/1843/critique-hpr/intro.htm.

Psychocinema

1 Jacques Lacan, *Le séminaire. Livre VII: L'éthique de la psychanalyse (1959–60)* (Paris: Seuil, 1986), p. 61.

2 Jacques Lacan, *The Seminar of Jacques Lacan: The Ethics of Psychoanalysis*, trans. Denis Porter (London: Routledge, 1997), p. 319.

3 G. W. F. Hegel, "The Phenomenology of Mind," available at www.marxists.org/reference/archive/hegel/works/ph/phprefac.htm.

4 G. W. F. Hegel, *The Phenomenology of Spirit*, trans. A. V. Miller (Oxford University Press, 1977), p. 383.
5 Melanie Klein, "Notes on Some Schizoid Mechanisms," *The International Journal of Psychoanalysis* 27 (1946), pp. 99–110.
6 Wilfred Bion, "A Theory of Thinking," *International Journal of Psychoanalysis* 42 (July–August 1961), pp. 306–10.
7 Wilfred Bion, *Learning from Experience* (London: Tavistock, 1962), p. 7.
8 Arthur Schopenhauer, *The World as Will and Representation*, Volume I, trans. Judith Norman, Alistair Welchman and Christopher Janaway (Cambridge University Press, 2010), p. 338.
9 Vakhtang Gomelauri (2018) "Can You Die of Shame?" Vakhtang Gomelauri LCSW [blog], available at https://vakhtanggomelaurilcsw.wordpress.com.
10 Todd McGowan, *Enjoying What We Don't Have: The Political Project of Psychoanalysis* (Lincoln: University of Nebraska Press, 2013).
11 Alenka Zupančič, *What IS Sex?* (Cambridge, MA: MIT Press, 2017), p. 97.
12 Todd McGowan, "The Universality of Non-Belonging," *The Philosopher* 108, 4 (Autumn 2020), pp. 54–60.
13 Dylan Moran, "Dylan Moran (BBC America Comedy Live Presents) Part 4 (Last)," YouTube, uploaded by John Hio, July 19, 2020, www.youtube.com/watch?v=Rgm4kwMs-Mc.
14 G. W. F. Hegel, "Part One of the Encyclopaedia of Philosophical Sciences: The Logic," available at

www.marxists.org/reference/archive/hegel/works/sl/slessenc.htm#:~:text.

15 Jacques Lacan, *The Seminar of Jacques Lacan Book XI: The Four Fundamental Concepts of Psychoanalysis*, ed. Jacques-Alain Miller, trans. Alan Sheridan (New York: W. W. Norton and Co., 1998), p. 139.

16 Sigmund Freud [1905], *Jokes and their Relation to the Unconscious*, trans. James Strachey (New York: Norton, 1960), pp. 137–8.

17 Groucho Marx, dir., *Duck Soup* (1933).

18 Jean-Paul Sartre, *Being and Nothingness: An Essay on Phenomenological Ontology*, trans. Hazel E. Barnes (London: Methuen, 1958), p. 60.

19 Barbara Creed, *The Monstrous-Feminine: Film, Feminism, Psychoanalysis* (London: Routledge, 2007), pp. 16–30.

20 Laura Mulvey, "Visual Pleasure and Narrative Cinema," *Screen* 16, 3 (Autumn 1975), pp. 6–18.

21 John Steinbeck, "A Primer on the '30s," *Esquire* (June 1960), pp. 85–93.

22 Lacan, *The Seminar of Jacques Lacan Book XI: The Four Fundamental Concepts of Psychoanalysis*, p. 103.

23 Jacques Lacan, "The Mirror Stage," in *Écrits: A Selection*, trans. Alan Sheridan (London: Routledge, 2005), p. 3.

24 Mulvey, "Visual Pleasure and Narrative Cinema," pp. 6–18.

25 Michel Foucault, *The Birth of the Clinic*, trans. A. M. Sheridan (London: Routledge, 2003), p. 89.

26 Hegel, "The Phenomenology of Mind."

27 Jacques Lacan, *Seminar XVII: The Other Side of*

Psychoanalysis, trans. Russell Grigg (New York: W. W. Norton & Co., 2008), p. 116.

28 Mladen Dolar, "On Rumours, Gossip and Related Matters," in *Objective Fictions: Philosophy, Psychoanalysis, Marxism*, ed. Adrian Johnston (Edinburgh University Press, 2022), pp. 144–64.

29 Jean Genet, *The Balcony* (London: Faber Finds, 2015).

30 Jacques Lacan, *Annexes au Séminaire, Livre XVII: L'envers de la psychanalyse* (Paris: Seuil, 1991), p. 239.

31 André Bazin, *Qu'est-ce que le cinéma?* (Paris: Cerf, 1976).

32 Noël Burch, *Theory of Film Practice*, trans. Helen R. Lane (Princeton University Press, 1981), p. 15.

33 Audre Lorde, *The Master's Tools Will Never Dismantle the Master's House* (London: Penguin, 2018).

34 Benjamin Studebaker, "Requiem for a Soldier," in *Four Essays on the Revolutionary Subject* (London: Everyday Analysis, 2024), p. 62.

35 Octave Mannoni, "I Know Very Well, but All the Same . . .," in *Perversion and the Social Relation*, ed. Molly Anne Rothenberg, Dennis A. Foster and Slavoj Žižek (Durham, NC: Duke University Press, 2003), pp. 68–92.

36 Ernst Bloch, *Atheism in Christianity: The Religion of the Exodus and the Kingdom*, trans. J. T. Swann (New York: Verso, 2009), p. viii.

37 Jacques Lacan, "Seminar XXI: Les non-dupes errent," available at https://nosubject.com/index.php?title=Seminar_XXI&oldid=48747.

38 Jean-François Lyotard, *Libidinal Economy*, trans.

Iain Hamilton Grant (London: Continuum Impacts, 2004).

39 Ian Parker, *Stalinist Realism and Identity* (London: Everyday Analysis, 2024).

40 Slavoj Žižek, *Freedom: A Disease without Cure* (London: Bloomsbury, 2023), p. 108.

Conclusion

1 Saint Anselm, *Proslogion*, trans. M. J. Charlesworth (University of Notre Dame Press, 1979), p. 54.